9.95
ETH

JEWISH UKRAINIAN RELATIONS

TWO SOLITUDES

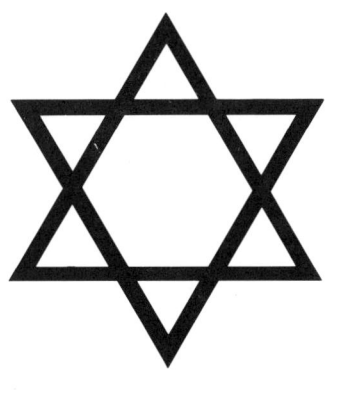

JEWISH-UKRAINIAN RELATIONS:

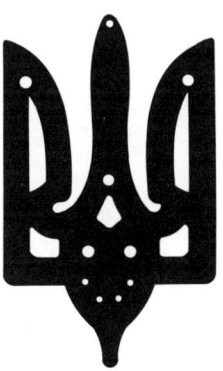

TWO SOLITUDES

Howard Aster & Peter J. Potichnyj

MOSAIC PRESS
Oakville — New York — London

CANADIAN CATALOGUING IN PUBLICATION DATA

Aster, Howard
    Jewish-Ukrainian relations

2nd rev. exp. ed.
Includes bibliographical references and index.
ISBN 0-88962-367-8

1. Jews - Ukraine - History. 2. Ukraine - Ethnic
relations - History. I. Potichnyj, Peter J.,
1930-   . II. Title.

DS135.R93U317 1987   947'.71004924   C87-094202-6

No part of this book may be reproduced or transmitted in any form, by any means, electronic or mechanical, including photocopying and recording information storage and retrieval systems, without permission in writing from the publisher, except by a reviewer who may quote brief passages in a review.

Published by Mosaic Press, P.O. Box 1032, Oakville, Ontario, L6J 5E9, Canada. Offices and warehouse at 1252 Speers Rd., Unit 10, Oakville, Ontario, L6L 5N9, Canada.

Published with the assistance of the Canada Council and the Ontario Arts Council.

First Edition published in 1983.

© Howard Aster & Peter J. Potichnyj, 1987, Revised second edition
Design by Rita Vogel
Typeset by Speed River Graphics
Printed and bound in Canada

ISBN 0-88962-367-8 paper

MOSAIC PRESS:

IN THE UNITED STATES:
   Riverrun Press Inc., 1170 Broadway, Suite 807, New York, N.Y., 10001, U.S.A.
IN THE U.K.:
   John Calder (Publishers) Ltd., 18 Brewer Street, London, W1R 4AS, England.

CONTENTS

INTRODUCTION TO A REVISED EDITION i
PREFACE 7
MODERNIZATION AND ITS IMPACT ON
    JEWISH-UKRAINIAN RELATIONS 49
A JEW AND A UKRAINIAN: AUTOBIOGRAPHICAL
    AFTERTHOUGHTS 71
INDEX 85

INTRODUCTION TO REVISED EDITION

The fate of intellectual projects cannot be anticipated with any degree of accuracy. The same way as one cannot predict the future course of human knowledge, likewise, one cannot foresee the outcomes of one's intellectual endeavours.

In 1983, on the urging of a number of colleagues, we put together the two academic essays we had written the previous year and published them as a monograph entitled *Jewish-Ukrainian Relations: Two Solitudes*. Like most academic monographs, we anticipated some small-scale concern with the topic, some few intellectual ponderings. Following the release of the monograph, we organized a conference on the topic of Jewish-Ukrainian relations and we edited the papers from that conference which will soon be released in book form entitled *Jewish-Ukrainian Relations in Historical Perspective*.

In the new years since the publication of our monograph, a range of academic inquiries have been launched into this area. Clearly, the topic is of a deep concern and preoccupation, mainly to Ukrainian scholars and academics, less so to Jewish scholars and academics. The reasons for this 'uneven development' within the Ukrainian and Jewish academic communities are complex. Some of the reasons are explored in our original essays. Other reasons have become more apparent to us recently.

What has surprised us is the reverberations of our efforts in circles outside the academic community. In August, 1985, in the No. 8 issue of *Vsesvit*, pp. 151-155, published in Kiev, there was a long review article of our monograph entitled "Khto i dlia choho 'perepysuie' istoriiu." The review was intriguing for many reasons, but mainly because our monograph was interpreted not only as a very serious theoretical but also a very serious practical problem.

Most of all, it was surprising for us to realize that we had addressed a topic which was deemed to be explosive and significant in Kiev. Rising to the challenge, we prepared and submitted a response. The response was never published in Kiev. However, we think that the response does summarize a range of opinions, views and preoccupations shared by not only both of us, but by many others as well. Here was our response:

February 12, 1986

Mr. Vitalii Korotych,
Editor-in-Chief,
"Vsesvit"
252021 Kiev - 21
34 Kirov Street,
Ukrainian SSR.

From the Edge of Fire: A Response to Vitalii Cherednychenko and Yevhen Sheremet, "Khto i dlia choho 'perepysuie' istoriiu, *Vsesvit*, No. 8, August, 1985, pp. 151-155.

In trying to sum up his life's work, one of the most important public figures of this century stated: "For us, the tasks of education in socialism were closely integrated with those of fighting. Ideas that enter the mind under fire remain there securely and for ever." The author of these lines is Leon Trotsky in *My Life*, chapter 35.

For us, this statement is true not only for education in socialism, but for education everywhere. There is no higher vocation than the struggle of ideas. Ideas are never apparent, or transparent. They require elaboration, formation and reformulation, exposition and application. If ideas were transparent or apparent, there would be no need for educators or intellectuals.

The struggle for truth, for objectivity, for clarity of ideas is something that every intellectual must aspire to. The "cathedral of knowledge" as Sir Karl Popper calls it, is never complete. No idea, no problem, no intellectual pursuit can ever be claimed to be totally resolved, forever. It is always possible to make an honest effort, to think through afresh, to undertake with renewed vigour, the accepted ideas of previous ages, or epochs. We are, indeed, the heirs to the truths of our fathers, but we need not be slaves to those truths. It is our responsibility to ensure that we examine, consider and assess all the inherited truths of our fathers.

It is, therefore, a great delight for us to learn of the deep interest the "Kievan comrades" have in our problem. It is also of deep delight to us that the authors have devoted six pages to an elaboration and scrutiny of our publication, *Jewish-Ukrainian Relations: Two Solitudes*. In Canada, we have the sense that we live between the two, great superpowers. What we do, what we think, what we undertake, we assume has a very limited audience. Hence, it is important to us that our efforts in this area have found their way to such a lengthy consideration by the leading Ukrainian journal, *Vsesvit*.

The authors of the review article share with us, to begin, a common belief. Both we and they believe that the question of Jewish-Ukrainian relations is a vitally important, perhaps, urgent, issue. They also agree with us that in recent times, over the past 6 years, there has been a serious and growing pre-occupation among various individuals and organizations to undertake a careful examination and reconsideration of this issue. Further, both we and the authors in Kiev believe that this is the first beginnings of what may likely evolve into a more elaborate and comprehensive effort at reconciliation between Jews and Ukrainians.

In this context, our book, *Jewish-Ukrainian Relations: Two Solitudes* is a preliminary mapping of the territory, a piece of intellectual archaeology. Much more needs to be done. Indeed, some time soon will see the publication of a more ambitious work, *Jewish-Ukrainian Relations in Historical Perspective*, edited by the two of us. This work, to be published by the Canadian Institute of Ukrainian Studies at the University of Alberta, is a collection of some 25 articles by noted scholars in the field, from a variety of disciplines and from various countries. No doubt, further works will be forthcoming.

But there is much more that separates us, alas! A long, point-by-point rebuttal is not necessary at this time. Perhaps, in the future, when the spirit of global collegiality would be possible, when scholars from the west and the east would be able to get together and discuss such matters as Jewish-Ukrainian relations in a spirit of co-operation, then both of us would be able to clarify our views more effectively. But until then, let us indicate a few significant points.

First, in our work on this thorny problem, we have not hidden anything. We have not distorted history. Indeed, we have indicated throughout our work the details of the unhappy and unfortunate events in the legacy of Jewish-Ukrainian relations. But we have gone further. We have also tried to formulate a series of perspectives, a manner of thinking about these events so that we can begin the difficult task of explaining these events. Our task was not to re-write history, but to approach the problematic question of 'How do we think about that history?' 'How to explain that history?' Why is this an important question? Because, in our view, the future of Jewish-Ukrainian relations depends upon our ability to think about and to think through the legacy of the past. We should not discount the past. But, at the same time, we should never, never, be bound by the past. All progressive minded people, including our critics in Kiev, would and should readily admit that we do make the future. The past is the burden which our fathers have given to us to bare. But the future remains for us to create!

Second, in the review article, we are labelled as 'zionists' and 'bourgeois nationalists.' Further, they go on to argue that it is only zionists and bourgeois nationalists who are able to talk to each other, assuming that other people are incapable of collegial discussions. Alas, these easy shibboleths or code-words betray not intellectual objectivity, but prejudicial and stereotyped thinking, the very qualities from which we are trying to free ourselves. In our work, we appeal to everyone's ability to go beyond the various 'idols' which haze thinking about the subject of Jewish-Ukrainian relations. It is clear that our opponents in Kiev have succumbed to their own form of idolatry — the idolatry of political and ideological polemics. In doing so, they distort our sincere efforts and they condemn any attempt at human rapprochement between two national groups.

Third, they have it wrong. We do not write encumbered by any masters or at the behest of any powers. We are free agents, able to express our views, even our iconoclastic views, on this subject. We serve no masters, we serve no ideological idols, we pay homage to no popular perspectives. Perhaps it is this freedom to shatter all idolatry which has pricked the ideological sensitivities of the comrades in Kiev.

Fourth, to suggest, as they do, that our preliminary exploration of Jewish-Ukrainian relations is a highly organized effort to develop a political programme and a common front aimed at the destruction of the Soviet Union — while it is very flattering — is surely an exaggeration. We do take ideas seriously. But ideas proposed to the public are a matter of open and frank discussion, not an ideological tool to be used by political powers.

Fifth, we do not deny that Jewish-Ukrainian relations have been beset by atrocities, tragedies, deaths, misfortunes. Our view is that these periods coincide with extended periods of internal turmoil in Ukraine. When peace and stability set in, even for a brief period, when Ukraine was able to set its own political agenda, develop its own political institutions, free from foreign influence, then harmonious relations between Jews and Ukrainians prevailed. Our "colleagues" refuse to acknowledge this point. To them, Jews and Ukrainians are wolves, at war with each other and death and tragedy are a necessary part of and endemic to Jewish-Ukrainian relations. Alas, we do not believe this. Indeed, history disproves their view.

Sixth, the ideological blinkers worn by our Kievan opponents disallow them from asking some serious questions about the nature of Jewish-Ukrainian relations. For example, is the cultural, political, economic and religious realities of contemporary Ukraine (or for that matter USSR) conducive to the development of Jewish and Ukrainian life today? Is it true that the best form of collaboration between Jews and Ukrainians today in the USSR takes place in the confines of the dissent movement, in political prisons? Why? The virulent criticism — alas, the fear — expressed by our critics in Kiev would be much stronger if contemporary realities conformed more to their portraits. But that is not the case. The evidence disproves their case.

Seventh, in our view, the only form of relations between Jews and Ukrainians which can lead to harmonious relationships are those based upon equality and freedom, for both nationalities. This is equally true in the west as it is in Ukraine, and in the USSR. History tells us that both national groups are capable of such harmonious relations, but only under the conditions of equality and freedom. We would hope that Kievan reviewers would accept this simple truth.

Finally, when we wrote our work we clearly identified ourselves as a Jew and a Ukrainian and we tried to articulate our views from this perspective. Probably for balance, the review of our work was written by two persons with "good" Ukrainian names. But their criticism is in the spirit of "grab 'em and hold 'em" ("tashshyt' i ne uskat' ") so well described by a Russian writer Gleb Uspenskii. Actually, one may have been enough because as the well-known Russain saying has it "Russkii um i russkii dukh, zady tverdit i lzhet za dvukh."

    Sincerely,
    H. Aster
    P. Potichny

If our preliminary work had some reverberations in Kiev, it also coincided with the work of the Deschenes Commission's Inquiry into War Criminals in Canada, a Commission of Inquiry launched in October 1985 and which reported in March 1987. This Commission of Inquiry provoked significant reactions both within the Jewish and Ukrainian communities in Canada. Again, the process by which a public inquiry devolved into a confrontation between Jews and Ukrainians in Canada is infinitely complex. However, what is clear is that the question of Jewish and Ukrainian relationships and relatedness remains a vital, provocative topic.

It is not easy to shed oneself of 1000 years of historical intimacy, even in the conditions of the 'new world,' such as in Canada, the United States, or Australia. In these and other countries, the questions associated with Jewish-Ukrainian relationships have assumed a higher profile in the past few years. Commissions of Inquiry in Canada and Australia, the activities of the OSI in the United States, the Demjanjiuk trial in Israel, these and other events have once again led Jews and Ukrainians to recognize that their historical legacies and contemporary realities — for better or worse — intersect. And, they intersect today in some most complex and varied ways. The issue of war criminals and the Demjanjiuk trial in Israel raise the question of justice as a parameter of concern in Jewish-Ukrainian relations. A thorny, difficult issue, but a vital one for both communities.

The history of Jews and Ukrainians in the twentieth century raises the reality of the Holocaust and what Robert Conquest, in his recent paragon work, has called the terror/famine. How do two people absorb, live through and beyond, or comprehend this premeditated assault upon their existence raises infinitely sensitive and horrific difficulties. Is the legacy of the twentieth century to be one which condemns future generations of Jews and Ukrainians to live with these historic realities into the next generations?

Amnesia, as psychiatrists would tell us, is one way in which the human psyche deals with the past. Among Jews and Ukrainians, there are some who would advocate this approach to the problem of Jewish-Ukrainian relations.

Collective guilt is another way in which relations between Jews and Ukrainians might be resolved. There are those who would advocate the affixing of collective guilt upon either the Jewish or the Ukrainian communities. Only through an act of the public admission of collective guilt could absolution from history be achieved. It would appear very unlikely that this will occur.

Continuing communal strife is another option open. For many people, this would appear to be the most likely anticipation of what the future may hold. The increased public sensitivity within each community to the issues that divide the communities makes one very sober to this likely outcome.

For many others, separate development, a closing off of contacts, turning inward, is the best response to the dilemma. If you cannot re-write history, why even attempt to make it comprehensible? It cannot be done. The fate of Jews and Ukrainians lies in communal disassociation, not association.

Clearly, in our view, none of these give us a way out. We believe that recognition, understanding, knowledge and mutual comprehension is what is now required by both Jews and Ukrainians.

The publication of this second revised edition of this monograph, we hope, can add some small measure to this process of mutual understanding.

H.A., P.P.
March 1987
Hamilton, Ontario

JEWISH-UKRAINIAN RELATIONS

PREFACE

It is not often that academics have the sense that they have uncovered an intellectual topic which is fundamentally novel, exciting, and previously unmined. In most instances, there are fundamentally sound reasons that certain intellectual problems tend to attract significantly large numbers of researchers. In the life of the academician, research tends to perpetuate research, one problem leads to another, one puzzle solved triggers the discovery of another puzzle to be solved. If one happens across an intellectual problem which has been relatively untouched in academic disciplines, then one tends to be sceptical about its academic value or the worth of devoting time and effort to its exploration.

It is within this context that the two essays collected in this monograph must be approached. The simple fact is that the topic of Jewish-Ukrainian relations is one of those intellectual problems which has not attracted much research or academic energy. When we first approached the topic, we faced a variety of significant problems — the relative paucity of research sources, the incoherence of almost any methodological approach which could provide a focus for research activity, the general intellectual scepticism with which our colleagues viewed our efforts in this area, the apparent ossified layers of prejudice and confused meanings which tainted the ability of two researchers, one Ukrainian and one Jewish, to approach this massive problem area and, finally, the interdisciplinary skills required to make sense of the topic.

The effort exerted in the preparation of these papers, on a personal level, has been most rewarding. Stepping into an intellectual minefield has many dangers, but it also has many rewards. We believe very firmly that the topic of Jewish-Ukrainian relations warrants much more attention, devotion and careful intellectual exploration than has been given to it in the past. It is also apparent to us, now, that there are some major implications of a theoretical, historical, personal and practical dimension which may emerge from a fuller devotion to this topic.

The two essays in this monograph were prepared for two learned societies conferences, one in June 1982 and one in September 1982. In response to the many comments, queries and the general level of public interest provoked by these two presentations, we have decided to bring them together into one small volume. These two essays should be regarded as preliminary, exploratory studies in this area. They are more like search-lights or beacons in an intellectual area shrouded by fog. Clearly, much more research, thought and effort will follow.

Howard Aster
Peter J. Potichnyj

Hamilton, Ontario
June, 1983

JEWISH-UKRAINIAN RELATIONS:
TWO SOLITUDES

INTRODUCTION

Canada is an interesting place from which to reflect upon Jewish-Ukrainian relations. Canadians have the advantage of being fundamentally detached from world history, remote from the ravages of war and turmoil and temperamentally dispassionate in the consideration of most things. Given the context with which discussions of Jewish-Ukrainian relations usually take place, it is perhaps just as well that we begin with the advantage of detachment, remoteness and dispassionateness. However, there is another reason as to why it is useful to begin a reconsideration of Jewish-Ukrainian relations from a Canadian perspective. One of the most powerful and obviously accurate insights into Canada has been provided by the novelist Hugh MacLennan, who, in a precisely crafted metaphor, suggested to us that the history of the relationship between French-Canada and English-Canada must be characterized as 'two solitudes'.[1] MacLennan's metaphor, probably more than any other, has been able to summarize a complex pattern of interaction, or lack of interaction, between English and French-Canadians in Canada. In looking at Canada within the notion of 'two solitudes', we see two people, with two distinctive languages and cultures, who, for a variety of historical accidents, ended up living in the same geographic territory which became known as Canada. Moreover, these two people, for a variety of historical reasons and accidents ended up shaping a common set of political institutions.

---

* Both authors are Professors of political science at McMaster University, Hamilton, Ontario, Canada.
We would like to thank Ms. Rachel Rempel for her invaluable assistance in compiling material for this paper.
[1] Hugh MacLennan, *Two Solitudes*, Toronto, Macmillan, 1945, and *The Other Side of Hugh MacLennan: Selected Essays Old and New*, Toronto, Macmillan, 1978.

In Canada we have recently come to recognize that the history of these two people, each one individually and in their own right, can be thematically characterized by the term 'survival'. The term 'survivance' has long been the rallying-cry of French-Canadian nationalists and has been reflected not only in the political and social writings of Quebec, but has also been a power element of thematic unity within the literature of Quebec.[2] However, it has only been identified, of late, as a major element of thematic unity within the literature of English-speaking Canada.[3] And yet, while there seems to be this commonality of thematic characterization which runs through the literature of these two people within Canada, their relationship has been portrayed as one of 'two solitudes'. When, indeed, they have come into close and intimate relations, usually, it has resulted in acrimony, strife, tension. Indeed, the writing of the history of the relationship differs dramatically and radically depending upon who writes it. The overwhelming portrait of the relationship from the French-Canadian perspective is one of total oppression, exploitation and almost tyrannical control by the English-Canadians of the French-Canadians.[4] Conversely, the portrait of the relationship from the English-Canadian perspective tends to be one of gentlemanly tolerance, continuous accommodation and extreme respect by English-Canadians of the French-Canadian fact.[5] There appears to be an in-

---

[2] The individual whose name is most often associated with the development of the notion of "survivance" is Abbé Lionel Groulx. Groulx was a professor of history at the University of Montreal, and in 1918 became editor of the monthly review *L'Action Française*. For over four decades Groulx's nationalistic ideas had a profound impact on the development of French-Canadian politics and literature. See for example: Jean-Pierre Gaboury, *Le Nationalisme de Lionel Groulx: Aspects Idéologiques*, Ottawa, Editions de l'Université d'Ottawa, 1970.

[3] See for example Margaret Attwood, *Survival*, Toronto, Anansi, 1971. As well the corpus of critical works by Northrop Frye is immensely important and influential. A recent critical article which undertakes a reexamination of the idea of the thematic unity of English-Canadian literature is Eli Mandel, "Strange Loops: Northrop Frye and Cultural Freudianism", in *Canadian Journal of Political and Social Theory*, Vol. V, No. 3, Fall 1981, pp. 33—42. Ronald Sutherland's work, *Second Image: Comparative Studies in Quebec/Canadian Literature*, Toronto, New Press, 1971 was the first critical study which compared English and French language literature in Canada. See also, Roland Sutherland, *The New Hero: Essays in Comparative Quebec/Canadian Literature*, Toronto, Macmillan, 1977.

[4] See for example René Levesque, *An Option for Quebec*, Toronto, McClelland and Stewart, 1968, Léandre Bergeron, *Petit Manuel d'histoire du Québec*, Montreal, Editions Québécoises, 1970, are perhaps the most obvious and overstated documents on this perspective. More recent works which carry forward this analysis are Henry and Sheilagh Hodgins Millner, *The Decolonization of Quebec: An Analysis of Left-Wing Nationalism*, Toronto, McClelland and Stewart, 1973. For another view see Dale Postgate and Kenneth McRoberts, *Quebec: Social Change and Political Crisis*, Toronto, McClelland and Stewart, 1980.

[5] This tradition of interpretation was first put forward by Mason Wade, *The French Canadians 1760—1945*, Toronto, Macmillan, 1956, and extended by Ramsay Cook, *Canada and the French Canadian Questions*, Toronto, Macmillan, 1970, and his *The Maple Leaf Forever, 1977*.

capacity to agree upon a common historical perspective, or even to the sharing of a common understanding of this history. As MacLennan put it so aptly, we in Canada live in a land of 'two solitudes'. In approaching a preliminary discussion of Jewish-Ukrainian relations, we would be well-served by bearing in mind the above considerations. History tends to present us with uniqueness. We are often driven to the point of thinking that historical events, or even extended relations in history between people, tend to be particular and without parallel. And, indeed, that is the case. However, it is also wise that we learn from historical similarities.

The problem of Jewish-Ukrainian relations has recently assumed a higher public profile as well as a higher academic importance. The context of this renewed interest in this problem is worth noting because it locates the problem of our concern in this paper in a contemporary situation and because it also identifies the parameters of the difficulties we confront. On September 27, 1981, *The New York Times Magazine* published an article entitled "Babi Yar's Legacy" by Lucy S. Dawidowicz. The author, in her treatment of the historical record surrounding the events of Babi Yar, presents a compelling argument. However, at the same time, Ms. Dawidowicz articulates a perspective on Jewish-Ukrainian relations which is commonly held; and that is the unfortunate tendency to characterize Ukrainians as inveterate anti-Semites.

> "The Jews were unprepared for abandonment and betrayal by those among whom they lived in peace for two decades. They were unprepared for the ease and speed with which some Ukrainians slipped back into the anti-semitism that had tainted Ukrainian history for centuries."[6]

As a statement about Jews' feelings towards their Ukrainian neighbours at this tragic moment in history there is truth in what Dawidowicz claims. It may well be true also that "some Ukrainians even rejoiced in misfortune of the Jews..."[7] What is deeply distressing is the author's ability to proceed to characterize an entire history of a people and their relationship to Jews as fundamentally "antisemitic".[8] The author further underlines this basic portrait of Ukrainians' attitudes towards Jews when she states "The Soviet dictatorship at first tried to restrain the Ukrainian antisemitism, though not out of love for the Jews... But after the German occupation of 1941, ancient prejudices were unloosed."[9] This statement is consistent with a general perception that historically Ukrainians have a deeply ingrained propensity towards anti-semitism and that during the German occupation anti-semitism simply acquired legitimacy. Other scholars have voiced similar arguments. For example:

---

[6] Lucy S. Dawidowicz, "Babi Yar's Legacy", *The New York Times Magazine*, September 27, 1981, p. 51.
[7] *Idem.*
[8] *Idem.*
[9] *Ibid.*, pp. 51—54.

> "Original anti-semitic feelings had been fanned by Nazi propaganda... John Fischer has pointed out that Ukrainian anti-semitism was stimulated by the inhabitants' fear they would have to return the property they had stolen from the Jews."
>
> "Whatever the weight one must give to the effects of the Nazi propaganda, there was no question that the Ukrainian population showed itself violently anti-semitic after the end of the war".[10]

Schwartz then goes on to quote from an account of a Russian Jew who left Kharkov in March 1944, returned at the end of the year and then in 1945 made his way to Palestine: "The Ukrainians received the returning Jews with open animosity... The Ukrainian authorities are openly anti-semitic... The official answer to all Jewish representations is that the anti-semitism with which the population has been infected by the Germans can only be uprooted gradually."[11]

The recent publication of Dawidowicz's article triggered a major reaction from the Ukrainian community in United States, Canada and various European countries.[12] The virulent reaction must be understood as emerging from two major events which preceeded the publication of the article in the *New York Times*.

First, there was the establishment of the Public Committee for Jewish-Ukrainian Cooperation in Jerusalem in 1979 and its subsequent splintering into the

---

[10] Harry Schwartz, "Has Russia Solved the Jewish Problem", *Commentary*, No. 2, February 1949, p. 132. See also Solomon M. Schwarz, "The New Anti-Semitism of the Soviet Union: Its Background and Its Meaning", *Commentary*, No. 5, 1949, pp. 535—545. On the question of the complicity of Ukrainians in German crimes see *The Standard Jewish Encyclopedia*, Garden City, N.Y.: Doubleday, 1966, p. 1852 and a more objective view is the *Universal Jewish Encyclopedia*, New York, 1943, Vol. 10, pp. 334—339. A very interesting symposium on the question of collaboration during World War II can be found in "Ukrainians in World War II: Views and Points", *Nationalities Papers*, Vol. X, No. 1, Spring 1982, pp. 1—39 in which several well-known scholars took part; Oleg Pidhaini, "Jews and Ukrainians in World War II", *The New Review*, No. 1, November, 1961, pp. 18—22; Leo Heiman, "Ukrainians and the Jews", *Ukrainian Quarterly*, No. 2, Summer 1961, pp. 107—116; Leo Heiman, "They Saved Jews: Ukrainian Patriots Defied Nazis", *Ibid.*, No. 4, Winter 1961, pp. 320—332; Joseph Tanenbaum, "The Einsatzgruppen", *Jewish Social Studies*, No. 17, January 1955, pp. 47—64.

[11] Harry Schwartz, *op. cit.*, pp. 132—133.

[12] See for example, "Antyukrains'ka paranoia", *Svoboda*, December 5, 1981, p. 2; A. Kaminskyi "V poloni kompleksu 'kolektyvnoii vyny'", *ibid.*, December 1, 1981, p. 2; I. Stebelskyi, "Babyn Iar i ukrainsko-zhydivski problemy", *ibid.*; M. Haliv, "Babyn Iar ukrainskymy i zhydivskymy ochyma", *Ibid.*, November 19, 1981, p. 4; "The 'Big Lie'," Editorial, *The Ukrainian Weekly*, No. 49, December 6, 1981, p. 6; "Babyn Iar i zlovmysna propaganda", *Novyi Shliakh*, No. 46, November 14, 1981; "Komu potribni spory z pryvodu trahedii Babynoho Iaru", *Vilne Slovo*, 1981; "Again, Revisionist History", Editorial, *The Ukrainian Weekly*, October 4, 1981, p. 6; "Again, 'Ukrainian Anti-semitism'", *Ibid.*, December 13, 1981, p. 6; "Ukrainian-Jewish Relations", *Ibid.*, December 27, 1981, pp. 7—8.

Society of Jewish-Ukrainian Relations in January 22, 1981.[13] In early 1981, Yakov Suslensky who had been involved in the organization of the Public Committee of Jewish-Ukrainian Cooperation in 1979 and then founded the Society of Ukrainian-Jewish Relations, visited North America and held high-level discussions with the leaders of both the Ukrainian and Jewish communities. A delegation of Ukrainian Americans also visited Israel at the invitation of the Israeli Government.[14]

Secondly the spiritual leaders of the Ukrainian Catholic Church Archbishop-Metropolitan Stephan Sulyk, the highest ranking Ukrainian Catholic leader in the United States and Rabbi Marc Tanenbaum, a leading American Rabbi and the national spiritual director of the American Jewish Committee, met on May 4th, 1981 in Philadelphia. The purpose of the meeting was to establish a direct line of communication between the two communities and to reaffirm their point of concerns for ecumenism in the spirit of Vatican Council II. Rabbi Tanenbaum is quoted to have stated "by leaving our dark past behind us, Jews and Ukrainians can do much together. In addition to the many joint efforts on local issues, now taking place in cities around the country, our two communities should continue to join hands especially in affirming religious and cultural human rights for Jews and Ukrainians now living in the Soviet Union".[15] This symbolic reapproachment between the religious leaders of Ukrainian Catholic Church and a Rabbi of the American Jewish Committee was widely reported and applauded in the Ukrainian press. It is worthwhile noting that in the Soviet Union the coincidence of these two events was reported and condemned in the Soviet Ukrainian press.[16]

---

[13] *The Programme of Action* of the Society of Jewish-Ukrainian Relations dated April 13, 1981 can be found in *The Ukrainian Weekly*, April 19, 1981, p. 7. See also, Sh. Spektor, "Nuzhen li 'Komitet Evreisko-Ukrainskogo Sotrudnichestva'." *Nasha Strana*, January 23, 1981 (against the Committee) and V. Kagan, "Nuzhny li Evreiam Druzia?", *Novoe Russkoe Slovo*, October 22, 1981 (in favour of the Committee); L. Volianska, "Zhurnal 'Kontakt' poiavliaetsia dali", *Svoboda*, December 3—4, 1981.

[14] See for example "Ukrainian-Jewish Relations. A Discussion", *The Ukrainian Weekly*, April 12, 1981, pp. 6, 12, and *Ibid.*, April 19, 1981, p. 6; "Iakiv Suslenskyi vidvidav UNS i Svobodu", *Svoboda*, April 15, 1981, p. 1; "Liudyna z velykoiu misiieiu v zhytti", Editorial, *Ibid.*, April 16, 1982, p. 2; G. B. Zarycky, "Suslensky, UNA-ers Discuss Ukrainian-Jewish Relations, *The Ukrainian Weekly*, April 10, 1981, pp. 1, 7, 12; "Laying the Groundwork", Editorial, *Ibid.*, p. 6; Suslensky Reports on First Meetings with Ukrainians, Jews in U.S.", *Ibid.* April 26, 1981, p. 3, and 11; W. Dushnyk, "Metropolitan Sulyk, Suslensky Meet", *Ibid.*, May 10, 1981, p. 1; R. Ilnytskyi, "Pro initsiatyvnu hrupu 'Ukrainsko-Ievreiskoho Tovarystva'", *Svoboda*, July 1, 1981, p. 2.

[15] "Top Jewish, Ukrainian Spiritual Leaders Meet in Philadelphia", *The Ukrainian Weekly*, May 17, 1981, p. 3; "A Historic Meeting: Sulyk and Tanenbaum", *Ibid.*, May 24, 1981, p. 3.

[16] See especially the Soviet Ukrainian Journal of humour and satire *'Perets'*, June 1981 and the reaction to this attack by the North American newspaper *Svoboda*. "Zabolilo", Editorial, *Svoboda*, August 15, 1981, p. 2; "Nationalist-Zionist Conspiracy", *The Ukrainian Weekly*, September 6, 1981 and *The Ukrainian Echo*, September 23, 1981,

The impetus to engage in the discussion and analysis of Jewish-Ukrainian relations has come primarily from the Ukrainian intellectual circles. There appears to be a deep sense of urgency on the part of the Ukrainian intellectual, at least, to examine the relationship between Jews and Ukrainians both in the historical and contemporary periods. While certain individuals, within the Jewish community may wish to engage in a consideration of this subject, there does not appear to be the same sense of urgency on a community basis to do so. Indeed, one might claim that there is a reluctance on the part of most segments within the Jewish community to undertake a consideration of Jewish-Ukrainian relations.

THE METHODOLOGICAL DILEMMA

In approaching our intellectual problem, it is clear that we confront a number of fundamental methodological problems. How can one consider a relationship between Jews and Ukrainians? Along what dimensions ought we to consider the relationship? In what context should the consideration take place? Clearly, the experience of two people and two cultures which shared a history within a certain geographic location over a very long period of time suggests many points of departure for intellectual considerations.

In our view, the first point of departure — which we reject — is the notion of national character. The term 'national character' and variations thereon, has been known for a long time. Nations, especially European nations, tend to have long and continuous histories and these nations tend to develop within their populations self-conscious awareness of their differences from other nations. In ordinary speech we often tend to talk about, for example, the difference between being a Canadian as opposed to being an European, or an American. Generally, we have in mind a complex set of attitudes, behaviour patterns and generalized outlooks which a certain population within one nation-state shares and which distinguishes it from those attitudes, behaviour patterns and generalized outlooks of another nation-state. The term 'national character' has acquired a specific meaning in social science. It is generally understood to mean the enduring personality characteristics and life styles found among the population of a specific nation-state. It obviously relates to some set of basic or fundamental cultural qualities of a given nation-state or relates to an underlying set of psychological traits which characterize that population. The relationship between culture and personality has led some individuals to try to develop the notion of 'basic personality' which characterizes the population of a certain nation-state and the concept of the 'modal personality' was further developed from this basic conception.[17]

---

p. 3; See also V. Iu. Ievdokimenko and V. O. Ihnatov, *Natsionalizm i Natsii*, Kiev, Naukova Dumka, 1981.

[17] Among the most important works on national character see, Ruth Benedict, *The Chrysanthemum and the Sword: Patterns of Japanese Culture*, Boston, Houghton-Mifflin, 1946; Ralph Linton, *The Cultural Background of Personality*, New York, Appleton, 1945;

While the notion of 'national character' had a certain legitimacy in the social sciences for a certain period of time, it has come under severe and sustained criticism since the 1950s. First, it is fundamentally simple-minded to argue that behaviour of people can be explained by some basic and omni-present psychological mechanism, such as 'national character'. Second, within any cultural group, one does find significant variation between personality types, cultural predispositions and behaviour patterns. No mono-casual approach can explain this variety. Third, 'national character' studies have tended to find rather simplistic explanations for very complex subjects. And, finally, 'national character' studies have tended to evade the questions of history.

In approaching the question of Jewish-Ukrainian relations, we have purposely chosen not to adopt the 'national character' approach. Many persons have, indeed, come close to adopting the idea, consciously, or inadvertently. We do not believe that there is something intrinsic to the personality or culture of Ukrainians which makes them, or does not make them positively or negatively inclined to Jews. We reject the quasi-national character argument that we noted in Dawidowicz earlier. Moreover, in our view, to be tempted into a 'national character' argument tends to obscure rather than illuminate our subject.

The eclipse of the significance of the concept of 'national character' as a useful explanatory and theoretical concept in the social sciences preceeded the rise of the concept of 'political culture'. The concept 'political culture' developed as an attempt to bridge the gap between microanalysis with its emphasis on the psychological interpretations of individual political behaviour and the level of macroanalysis which tends to focus upon political sociology variables. The term 'political culture' has acquired a substantial reputation in the social sciences for a variety of reasons. First, it tends to bring together psychological and sociological concepts and to use them for the understanding of political behaviour. Second, it tends to be a useful way of doing comparative analysis. Third, it tends to direct social scientists into considerations of cultural phenomena and the process of socialization whereby individual learns the modalities of cultural objects.[18]

While the concept 'political culture' has acquired a degree of legitimacy in social science, it also has been subject to a number of major criticisms. First, it appears to be a marginal improvement over the notion of 'national character' — but not a radical improvement. In basing explanations on fundamentally psycho-

---

Margaret Mead, "National Character", in *Anthropology Today: An Encyclopedic Inventory*, edited by A. L. Kroeber, Chicago, University of Chicago Press, 1953, pp. 642—647, and perhaps the most important work by Geoffrey Gorer and John Rickman, *The People of Great Russia: A Psychological Study*, New York, Norton, 1962.

[18] The most famous work is by Gabriel A. Almond and Sidney Verba, *The Civic Culture: Political Attitudes and Democracy in Five Nations*, Princeton, Princeton University Press, 1963; Lucian W. Pye and Sidney Verba, eds., *Political Culture and Political Development*, Princeton, Princeton University Press, 1965, and Gabriel A. Almond and Sidney Verba, eds., *The Civic Culture Revisited*, Boston, Little Brown and Co., 1980, especially Chapter 1.

logical variables, it tends to obscure the complexity of cultural and political phenomena. Second, while it has a certain immediate appeal as an explanatory device, it tends to be used with such ease and imprecision that in trying to explain everything, it explains nothing. In effect it tends towards tautology. Third, the concept 'political culture' tends to be a-historical. By that we mean that the 'political culture' of any nation in its present configuration is the product of a complex and long historical development and that development is intricately related to various institutional changes, historical accidents or transformations, changes in the external environment, etc. The notion 'political culture' as it is presently used fails to incorporate these ideas. In view of these difficulties, we have chosen not to adopt the 'political culture' approach as a basis for the consideration of our problem.

How then to proceed? We have chosen to proceed rather simply. As a first approach, we want to consider the question of Jewish-Ukrainian relations from the point of view of the perspective of the Ukrainian and then from the point of view of the perspective of the Jew. Our notion of a perspective requires some clarification.

Our sense of a perspective relates to the way in which one achieves an understanding of a complex problem through the process of relating the parts one to another so that one arrives at a comprehension of the whole. The notion of a perspective is the position from which one perceives, assesses and judges the relative importance of facts, ideas, feelings, etc., and the consequence thereof, that is, our ability to understand or comprehend those facts, ideas, feelings etc. The notion of 'position' is not simply a consequence of economics or sociology, or history, or culture. It includes them all. Hence, the notion of perspective, to us is necessarily an inter-disciplinary notion and must draw upon the insights from a wide variety of fields, including history, politics, folklore, psychology, economics, etc. Moreover, while we may suggest that the notion of a perspective positions an individual from which his/her understanding may emerge, we also want to claim that a perspective is something shared by people and groups. We also conceive of the notion of perspective as something which changes over time, it is not static. These changes result from the alterations in the historical environment in which people live and the transformations in which people articulate their environmental and experiential circumstances. In suggesting that we approach our subject matter from the point of view of the perspectives of Ukrainians and Jews, we are careful to avoid the lapse into 'national character' arguments.

It is often thought that the unequivocal determination of 'the facts' can resolve the question of differing perspectives. Or, to put it in other terms, it is sometimes thought that history and historical scholarship can reveal to us the correct set of facts such that all persons who wish to adopt a perspective on a particular subject matter may be able to agree. In approaching the question of

Jewish-Ukrainian relations, there has been an effort to resolve the differing perspectives of Jews and Ukrainians by getting the historical record straight.

In the past number of years we have been subjected to a very intense effort of this sort. A number of historians have dealt with specific periods of Ukrainian history. They have attempted to use the "historical record" in order to resolve the question of differing perspectives. For example, Taras Hunczak in an article entitled "A Reappraisal of Simon Petliura and Jewish-Ukrainian Relations, 1917-1921", undertakes a very careful analysis of Jewish-Ukrainian relations 1917-1921 using a host of primary and secondary sources.[19] He concludes on the basis of his historical evidence that "In view of the evidence presented, the frequently repeated charge that Petliura was anti-semitic is absurd... Equally absurd is the attempt to establish Petliura's complicity in the pogroms against Ukrainian Jewry".[20] He further claims that "In view of the evidence presented in this paper, to convict Petliura for the tragedy that befell Ukrainian Jewry is to condemn an innocent man and to distort the record of Ukrainian-Jewish relations".[21]

Zosa Szajkowski in his article entitled: "A Reappraisal of Simon Petliura and Ukrainian-Jewish Relations, 1917—1921, A Rebuttal", states: "In my opinion, Professor Hunczak's paper should not have been published in a Journal of serious Jewish scholarship... The paper is not based on thorough research; it is rather a journalistic propaganda article, written by a man who is familiar neither with general Ukrainian history nor with its specific Ukrainian Jewish aspect".[22] Szajkowski's charge against Hunczak's poor historical scholarship is based upon his statement that "Yiddish and Hebrew sources are completely ignored by Professor Hunczak. In fact, the most important and complete history of the pogroms during Petliura's regime is either unknown to him or ignored. I refer to Ellias Tcherikower's book".[23] He concludes his article with the unequivocal statement based upon his irreproachable historical evidence that,

> "the critical utilization of both Ukrainian and Jewish sources condems Petliura for his role in leading and sanctioning the anti-Jewish pogroms in Ukraine. Of this terrible truth there can be no doubt."[24]

---

[19] Taras Hunczak, "A Reappraisal of Simon Petliura and Jewish-Ukrainian Relations. 1917—1921", *Jewish Social Studies*, July 1969, pp. 163—183.
[20] *Ibid.*, pp. 182—183. For an interesting article on V. Zhabotynskyi see: Izrajil Kleiner, "Die Jüdisch-Ukrainischen Beziehungen: Zum 100. Geburtstag von Volodymyr Żabotynskyj" *Mitteilungen*, No. 17, 1980, pp. 229—240.
[21] *Ibid.*, p. 183.
[22] Zosa Szajkowski, "A Reappraisal of Simon Petliura and Ukrainian-Jewish Relations, 1917—1921, A Rebuttal", *Jewish Social Studies*, July 1969, p. 184.
[23] *Idem.*
[24] *Ibid.*, p. 213. See also, Yaroslav Bilinsky, "Review Article: Ukrainians and Jews", *The Annals of the Ukrainian Academy of Arts and Sciences in the U.S. Inc.*, Volume XIV, No. 37—38, 1978—1980, pp. 244—257; W. Dushnyk, "Anti-Semitism and Ukraine", *Ukrainian Quarterly*, No. 1, Spring 1978, pp. 40—53.

Which historical record is correct? Can one expect historical evidence to resolve the dispute between Hunczak and Szajkowski? Or are we not faced with the dilemma that the reading of history by these two historians is based upon two radically different perspectives?

In our view the question of Jewish-Ukrainian relations obviously must include an historical discussion. However, the critical reading of history reveals for us the fact that we are dealing with two different perspectives. It may be that there is a "common history" but that "common history" is not read in the same manner, or that "common history" does not speak with the same voice to Jews and Ukrainians.

If we may argue that historical evidence does not resolve the questions of differing perspectives, are we thrown back to an argument that perspectives are nothing more but another term for stereotypes?

The term stereotype and its use in the social sciences is commonly attributed to Mr. Walter Lippmann and his book entitled, *Public Opinion*.[25] It is interesting to note that Lippmann starts with a long quotation from the VIIth book of Plato's Republic, the parable of the cave. Clearly Lippmann accepted Plato's parable as an example of what he himself had in mind by using the term stereotype, that is pictures or images in our heads or minds which give us an erroneous portrait of reality. The term stereotype, as Lippmann and others have used it, refers to pictures in our head, images, prejudices, codes, illusions, preconceptions, myths, belief, or fixed impressions. Whatever the term used, they all mean to imply that all human beings suffer from "constraints on human observation, arising overwhelmingly from the preestablished notions of our immediate or wider social and cultural surroundings, and from which we may only escape sometimes and then with the utmost exertion."[26]

The problem which the notion of stereotypes forewarns us has been known for centuries. We all are the victims of preconceptions or public knowledge which deeply affects the way in which we view others and the world. Francis Bacon in the early 17th century, differentiated between four types of constraints or false beliefs which affected human observations. First are the Idols of the Tribe, which "have their foundation in human nature itself, and in the tribe or race of men ... and the human understanding is like a false mirror, which, receiving rays irregularly, distorts and discolours the nature of things...".[27] The second are the Idols of the Cave, because "For everyone (besides the errors common to human nature in general) has a cave or den of his own... Owing either to his own proper and peculiar nature; to his education and conversation

---

[25] Walter Lippmann, *Public Opinion*, New York, Macmillan, 1922.

[26] Martin Brouwer, "Idola Fori or Some Social Aspects of Stereotypes and Their Development" an unpublished paper presented to the Fourth Annual Scientific Meeting (Mannheim, June 1981) of the International Society of Political Psychology, p. 1. 8.

[27] Francis Bacon, *The New Organon*, Indianapolis, Bobbs-Merril, 1960, Aphorisms, Book I, No. XLI.

with others; or to the reading of books, and the authorities of those whom he esteems and admires...".[28] The third are the Idols of the Market Place, because "For it is by discourse that men associate... and therefore the ill and unfit choice of words wonderfully obstructs the understanding. Nor do the definitions or explanations wherewith in some things learned men are want to guard and defend themselves, by any means set the matter right."[29] The fourth are the Idols of the Theatre. These are "Idols which have immigrated into men's minds from the various dogmas of philosophers, and also from wrong laws of demonstration. These I call the idols of the theatre, because in my judgement all the received systems are but so many stage plays, representing worlds of their own creation after an unreal and scenic fashion."[30]

In our view Jewish-Ukrainian relations exemplify all four of Bacon's idols!

The purpose of this paper is not to suggest a therapeutic manner in which Jews and Ukrainians can overcome their *idola*. Nor is the purpose of this paper to bring forward unbiassed evidence to buttress or rebuke these *idola*. Rather our purpose is to outline the manner, character and quality from which Ukrainians view Jews and Jews view Ukrainians. At most we can identify and perhaps offer some explanations of the dominant perspectives whereby these two people view each other.

In order to explicate the natures of these two perspectives adequately one would have to be a "Rennaissance man", thoroughly knowledgeable in the fields of history, psychology, literature, folklore, economics etc., not only from a Ukrainian but a Jewish perspective as well. We realize that we are not adequate to the task we set ourselves. We do hope though that we can at least identify a number of central factors which affect the nature of these two perspectives.

JEWS IN UKRAINE: AN HISTORICAL OVERVIEW

The earliest records of Jews in Ukrainian territories date back to the Second Century A.D. They came to Crimea and the eastern shore of the Black Sea long before Christianity was introduced into the region. These Bosphorus and Middle Eastern Jews who were highly hellenized, left behind them many inscriptions in Hebrew that date to this period.[31]

From Crimea and the *Caucasus* Jews moved into the lower Volga and Don regions where the Khazar State, founded by Turkic tribes, existed from the 7th to the 10th centuries. Around 740 Kahan Bulan and the Khazar elite accepted Judaism as the state religion.

---

[28] *Ibid.*, No. XLII.
[29] *Ibid.*, No. XLIII.
[30] *Ibid.*, No. XLIV.
[31] See *Entsyklopediia Ukrainoznavstva: Slovnykova Chastyna*, V. Kubiiovych, ed., Vol. II, 1955, pp. 670—680.

The Khazar state ceased to exist shortly after its defeat by the Kiev prince Sviatoslav in 964. The Jews then migrated back to Crimea, the Caucasus and even into Rus'-Ukraine.

In 987 Khazarian Jews proposed to Grand Duke Vladimir the Great of Kiev that he accept conversion to Judaism. The Chronicle describes how Prince Vladimir had presented to him arguments from representatives of three different religions — Byzantine Christianity, Roman Christianity and, significantly, Judaism.

The presence of Jews in the court of Prince Vladimir having a status equal to the Byzantine and Roman representatives suggests that Judaism was a significant force. In fact there are records that Kievan Metropolitan Ilarion in his sermons carried on polemics with the Jews.

During the 11th and 12th centuries Jews lived in Kiev where they had a separate district called "Zhydove" (1124) and there existed a separate Jewish Gate leading to that district. At that time the Jews were primarily traders and financiers. Consequently they were involved and responsible for certain administrative and financial functions for princes' protection. In 1113 there occurred a general upheaval of the population and revolt against Prince Sviatopolk. During this revolt Jews were persecuted as well as other money lenders. Accordingly to Hrushevskyi the direct pretext for this upheaval was the shortage of salt in Kiev due to the War in Volhynia. The Monk Prokhor began to distribute salt free of charge. Prince Sviatopolk confiscated the supply of salt and sold it at high prices. Since he was the protector of the Jews, after his death, the Kievans rebelled, killed several high courtiers and also the Jews.[32]

This is the first record of a "pogrom" against the Jews in Ukrainian territories. Some historians suggest that during this period the Jews in Ukraine did not differ either in dress or language from the general population. Differences emerged only when there occurred an immigration into the region of Jews from Western Europe.[33] It is interesting to note that a Soviet handbook about Kiev mentions these upheavals but makes no specific mention of the Jews.[34]

It is worth noting that during the same era Jews endured organized hardships in the other lands of Europe. In this Ukrainian region they did acquire positions of importance and for example Danylo, King of Halych-Volhynia enlisted Jewish assistance in reorganizing his state. As well, it is recorded that the Jews of the region lamented the death of Prince Vladimir Vasylkovych (1288) as the "destruction of the Temple".[35]

---

[32] Mykhailo Hrushevskyi, *Istoriia Ukrainy-Rusy*, New York, Knyhospilka, 1955, Vol. II. p. 290.
[33] *Ibid.*, Vol. V, p. 254.
[34] *Kyiv: Entsyklopedychnyi Dovidnyk*, Kiev, URE, 1981.
[35] M. Hrushevskyi, *op. cit.*, Vol. III, p. 105. His critical comments on the literature are found in Vol. V, pp. 651—653. Also see his *Istoriia Ukrainskoii Literatury*, New York, 1950, Vol. V, pp. 73—89.

The region was beset by a period of turmoil which extended from the fall of Kiev and Halych and annexation by Lithuania and Poland.

Between the 14th and 16th centuries, Volhynia, Kiev and Podolia was annexed by Lithuania. The result was that the Jews received the same privileges as the Jews had in the Lithuanian Principality.

From the end of the 14th century, the Jews began to arrive in Ukraine from Germany via Poland. The largest number of them arrived at the end of the 15th century when Poland-Lithuania accepted the Jews who were expelled by the German Emperor Maximillian I. It is of great significance that the emigration of the Jews from the West coincides with the decline of the independent Rus'-Ukrainian principalities. During this period the Jews began to use Yiddish as their language, to wear different clothing and lived in separate ghettos. The Jews had their rights codified in the so-called Lithuanian Statutes of 1529, 1566, and 1589. In Galicia the Jews had their rights and privileges codified in a Statute of 1334 issued by Casimir the Great. According to Lithuanian Statutes, the Jews had their own separate communities, the "Kahals", their own courts for internal Jewish problems and mixed courts for Jewish-Christian problems. Lithuanian Statutes placed Jews on an equal footing with nobility. The penalty for killing a Jew was the same as for killing a nobleman. The only restriction on Jews was that they were forbidden to use Christians as slaves. The supreme administrative organ was the "Council of Great Poland, Little Poland, Red Rus' and Volhynia" and the "Council of Lithuania". These councils met annually in "Vaads" and decided all of their religious, cultural and financial questions.

After the Union of Lublin (1569), colonization of Jews into Ukrainian lands expands. At the end of the 16th century Jews are found in 79 towns, some 25,000 people. Their occupation continues to be trade, financial operations and renting of lands and enterprises. Jews replaced Armenians from these trades.

During the 17th and 18th centuries Jews continued to be associated with the Polish ruling class. This close association had potential danger for the Jews and, indeed, the Jewish diets occasionally expressed concern over this matter. There were sporadic uprisings against the Polish rulers at the end of the 16th and the beginning of the 17th century. The Pavluk rebellion of 1637 had a localized character. The major large scale rebellion occurred in 1648 led by Bohdan Khmelnytsky. This Ukrainian uprising lasted from 1648 to 1654 and engulfed the entire Ukrainian region.

The Jews occupied a very precarious position at the beginning of the rebellion. As Walter Dushnyk states in his article entitled "Ukrainian-Jewish Relations on a Critical Path", quoting from Simon Dubnow's famous *History of the Jews in Russia and Poland:*

> "...'The only secure nest of the Jewish people and the legitimate seat of its national hegemony' achieved largely either by influencing the Polish governing circles and/or by uniting themselves in a firmly organized scheme of self-government. Enormous

> estates in Ukraine were in the hands of feudal Polish landlords, who, as human beings will, sought to relieve their consciences over their truly unconscionable treatment of the Ukrainian serf by regarding them as an inferior race. The management of these far flung estates was in the hands of stewards and *arendars* (loosely, rent collectors). Among these *arendars* were, according to Jewish sources, many Jews, who principally leased from the *PANS* (landlords) the right of 'propanations', or the sale of spiritus liquors. These leases had the effect of transferring to the Jews some of the powers over the Ukrainian serfs which were wielded by the noble landlords."³⁶

Dushnyk goes on to argue that the fact that the Jews were an instrument of domination over Ukrainians not only explains the devastation of Jewish communities during the Khmelnytsky uprising but also has conditioned Ukrainian perceptions of the Jews in subsequent eras.

> "Ukrainians have come to believe that the Jews, if not actual allies of Ukraine's historical enemies in its struggle for liberation, then at the very least are invaluable *instrument* — that is, indispensable *intermediaries* between the alien oppressors of Ukraine and the oppressed Ukrainian people."³⁷

During this period, according to the *Ukrainian Encyclopaedia* relying on Jewish sources somewhere between 100,000 to 180,000 Jews perished.³⁸ Dushnyk argues that:

> "...the Jews were literally caught in the middle among Ukrainians, Poles and Muscovites (today's Russians), the demise of 100,000 to, possibly, 200,000, of the Jews (according to Jewish Chroniclers). The Eastern European Jew of the time found himself between hammer and anvil: between landlord and serf, between Polish Catholic and Ukrainian and Muscovite Greek-Orthodox, and between Pole and Muscovite. This tragedy, at bottom, was that there was no place to go."³⁹

One way in which Jews could save themselves from this devastation was to accept Christianity and convert. Those who did so continued to be traders or financiers. Some of them eventually became cossack leaders and rose in the ranks of the *Starshyna* like for example M. Borokhovych (1687—1704), the Colonel of Hadiach or P. Hertsyk (1675—1695), the Colonel of Poltava, whose daughter married Hetman Philip Orlyk. The daughter of Mark Avramovych

---

³⁶ Walter Dushnyk, "Ukrainian-Jewish Relations On a Critical Path", *Ukrainian Quarterly*, No. 3, 1978, p. 229.
³⁷ *Ibid.*, 230.
³⁸ *Entsyklopediia Ukrainoznavstva*, *op. cit.*, p. 671; *Encyclopedia Judaica* Jerusalem, Keter Publishing House, 1971, Vol. XV, pp. 1513—1519.
³⁹ W. Dushnyk, "Ukrainian-Jewish...", *op. cit.*, pp. 229—230.

became the wife of Hetman I. Skoropadsky. This Avramovych family, known later as the Markovych family, produced a number of prominent Ukrainian cultural and political leaders. The Ukrainian legal statute of 1743 recognized as nobles those Jews who accepted Christianity voluntarily.[40]

After a period of a century of relative peace and reconstruction the Jewish community in 1768 was caught, once again, in the *Haidamak* uprisings known as "Koliivshchyna". The Ukrainians were striving to renew their independence while the Poles were attempting to impose "Catholicism on Orthodox Ukrainians, and the Russians were eager to put Ukrainian Catholics into the Orthodox church. In this prolonged struggle, many Poles and many Ukrainians were killed and, of course, many Jews lost their lives, too."[41] The Ukrainian Encyclopaedia estimates that between 50,000 and 60,000 Jews perished during the "Haidamak" uprisings.[42]

Peter the Great did not allow Jews to live in Hetmanshchyna (Left-Bank Ukraine) by his Ukaz of 1721. His followers, by their Ukazes of 1727, 1738, 1740 and 1742, sought to continue this policy. However, Hetman's administration, under pressure from Cossack *Starshyna*, did not fully implement these orders. But only about 600 Jews lived there anyway.[43]

In Zaporozhian Sich, Jews lived as traders but only in 1772 did they receive the right to trade in the Sich bazaar. Up to that time they had to trade outside the fortress.

In Slobozhanshchyna Jews were occupied primarily with wholesale trade but their numbers were also very small.

In Right-Bank Ukraine, the number of Jews was large. There, the Treaty of Andrusovo (1667) which partitioned Ukraine between Poland and Russia, provided for the return of the status quo prior to 1648. The Jews, therefore, returned to their traditional occupations — trade, financial operations, *arenda*, etc. But there was also the beginning of greater interest in trades, shoemaking, tailoring, goldsmithing and industry such as milling, ironmaking, etc.

After the partition of Poland at the end of the 18th century most of the Jews, some 900,000, became subjects of the Russian Empire. It was then that the "Pale of Settlement" was established to keep Jews out of Russia proper and Hetmanshchyna. Catherine II, in 1769, allowed them to live in southern Ukraine (Novorossiiskaia Gubernia) and the Ukaz of 1785 gave Jews equal status with the Christian population in that region.

In the 19th and beginning of the 20th century Jews lived primarily in Right-Bank Ukraine. The position of Jews in the Russian Empire depended on the category of population to which they belonged. For example, the Karaites from

---

[40] *Entsyklopediia Ukrainoznavstva, op. cit.,* p. 671.
[41] Stephan T. Possony, "The Ukrainian-Jewish Problem: A Historical Retrospect", *Ukrainian Quarterly,* No. 2, Summer 1975, pp. 141—142.
[42] *Entsyklopediia Ukrainoznavstva, op. cit.,* p. 671.
[43] *Idem.*

1863 were equal with Christians. The so-called "Polish Jews" were limited in various ways while "foreign Jews", from 1824 on, could not migrate into the Empire at all. However, tradesmen, industrialists and various specialists could receive special dispensations from the Tsarist government. In 1870 in Volhynia, Kiev and Podolia regions there were also 56 Jewish agricultural colonies with some 14,000 people. From 1844 the old "Kahal" organization was forbidden and the ancient internal Jewish autonomy was eliminated. In the 19th and the 20th centuries we also see the pauperization of Jewish masses as a result of large population increases, competition from non-Jews and various governmental restrictions. The end of the 19th and the beginning of the 20th century are marked by pogroms. The first pogrom in Odessa took place in 1871. In 1903—1905 a new wave of pogroms took place and all of them were organized by Russian chauvinist Black Hundreds.

In Austria-Hungary Jews received equality with other populations only in 1860. In Ukrainian lands they continued in their traditional professions with only 5—10 per cent involved in agriculture. Ukrainian villages were almost completely under Jewish economic and financial control. The monopoly of propination was also in Jewish hands. In 1870—1900 the development of the Boryslav oil fields was predominantly in Jewish hands.

The rural Ukrainian population began to develop itself culturally and economically only in the early 20th century. The cooperative movement which grew in the first half of the 20th century was important in this process.

At the beginning of the 20th century in Austria-Hungary some political cooperation took place between Ukrainian and Jewish political parties. In 1907 two Jewish deputies to the Vienna Parliament were elected by Ukrainian voters with the understanding that they were to support Ukrainian demands.[44]

In the Russian Empire, during 1917—1920, Jews did not have a single political orientation. They belonged to various oppositionist groups. In Ukraine, they had their own political parties — Zionists, Poalei-Zion, Bund, Jewish Workers Party, Jewish People's Party, or they took part in Russian political parties. In Ukrainian parties, with the exception of A. Margolin, and Z. Margulis (in the Ukrainian Party of Social Federalists) and J. Hermaize in the Ukrainian Social Democratic Workers' Party) there were almost no Jews.

Jewish parties entered the Ukrainian Central Rada in July 1917 where 30 places were reserved for them in the "Large" Council and 5 places in the "Little" Council. Also in the General Secretariat and later on in the Council of Ministers of the Ukrainian People's Republic there were several Jewish politicians such as M. Zilberfarb, M. Rafes, O. Zolotarev, A. Revutsky, Ia. Vulf-Liatsky, P. Krasnyi, S. Goldelman and others.

On January 8, 1918 the Ukrainian Central Rada passed the law establishing national-personal autonomy which in its liberal treatment of Jews was unpre-

---

[44] *Ibid.*, p. 673.

cedented.⁴⁵ Yiddish was recognized as the official language. Jewish schools were established including the Chair of Jewish History and Literature in the University of Kamenets-Podolsk. The government of the Ukrainian Peoples Republic had the Ministry of Jewish Affairs, alongside which there existed the Jewish National Council.

During the Revolution a wave of pogroms took place in Ukraine in which everybody was implicated: White Russian armies persecuted Jews, Bolsheviks persecuted wealthy Jews, Anarchists under Makhno did the same, Ukrainian guerillas and even regular military formations also attacked Jews. The Ukrainian government tried to prevent pogroms but was not very successful.

In Galicia, the Jews were neutral in the Polish-Ukrainian conflict but remained loyal to the Government of the Western Ukrainian People's Republic. They refused to send delegates to the Ukrainian People's Council. However, many of them served in the Ukrainian Galician Army (UHA) within which there existed even a "Jewish Battalion". In the territory controlled by the UHA and Sich Sharpshooters no pogroms took place. But when Ukrainian forces retreated from Lviv, the Poles attacked the Jews in November 1918 for being pro-Ukrainian.⁴⁶

After the Revolution in the Ukrainian SSR in 1925, Jews comprised 25 per cent of the party and government officials. In economic and financial establishments they comprised 26.7 per cent.

There was also an "agrarization" movement. Between 1924—1930 some 162 Jewish colonies were established with 9,526 households. In 1933 about 80,000 Jews were still in agriculture. The collectivization of agriculture and World War II destroyed them all. The Ukrainian Encyclopaedia reports that some foreign Jewish organizations supported the "agrarization" movement with a view of establishing a Jewish Homeland in Ukrainian territory. Such organizations as Agro-Joint evidently financed this effort. This movement ended in Ukraine in 1938. Other centers of Jewish colonization became Birobidzhan.⁴⁷

In 1930, in the Ukrainian SSR, there existed 3 Jewish National Areas: 1) Kalinindorf near Kherson comprising 32 Jewish Villages and 8 with mixed populations, 2) Novyi Zlatopil with 40 Jewish and 5 Ukrainian villages, 3) Stalindorf near Kryvyi Rih with 11 villages. In 1931 in north Crimea Freidorf was founded.⁴⁸

In Ukrainian lands in Poland, Romania and Czechoslovakia the situation of the Jews didn't change radically from the prewar period. But they lost their trade monopoly. The Ukrainian cooperative movement was especially strong

---

⁴⁵ See for example Solomon I. Goldelman, *Jewish National Autonomy in Ukraine 1917—1920*, Chicago, Ukrainian Research and Information Institute, 1968. Also see Panas Fedenko, "Arnold Margolin und die Ukrainische Nationale Wiedergeburt", *Mitteilungen*, No. 13, 1976, pp. 59—65.
⁴⁶ *Entsyklopediia Ukrainoznavstva*, op. cit., p. 673.
⁴⁷ *Ibid.*, pp. 673—674.
⁴⁸ *Idem.*

and competed with the Jews. On the political front, there was some cooperation between Jews and Ukrainians. On the whole, however, the Jews were loyal to existing regimes which were considered foreign by Ukrainians.

World War II was the period of total destruction of Ukrainian Jewry by the Nazis. The Ukrainian population with the exception of criminal elements did not participate in this genocide. There are many known instances of aid to the Jews even in the face of the death penalty meted out by the Germans. Metropolitan A. Sheptytsky, the Primate of the Ukrainian Catholic Church, issued a special pastoral letter in defense of Jews and sheltered many of them in monasteries. Several Jewish physicians are reported to have served in the Ukrainian Insurgent Army during 1943-1945. It is, nevertheless, an incontrovertible fact that the Ukrainian nationalist underground did not make a public stand in defense of the Jews. The Second Grand Assembly of the Organization of Ukrainian Nationalists of April 1941 which met in Cracow specifically labelled the Jews as the "tool of Moscow."[49] The Third Extraordinary Grand Assembly of the OUN, however, which took place, August 21—25 1943, in Ukraine, introduced important changes into the structure and the political programme of this organization in the direction of greater democracy and declared itself in defence of religious freedom, and in support of all national minorities and their cultural development.[50] The programme does not mention any specific nationality by name but one can assume that the above provisions applied also to Jews.

After World War II, the number of Jews in Ukraine became much smaller, some 800,000. The Soviet official policy supported wholesale assimilations of Jews. There was no attempt to revive either the Jewish national areas or Jewish cultural institutions. Many of Jewish activists became accused of "bourgeois nationalism" or "cosmopolitanism." These antisemitic tendencies were and continue to be supported officially by way of anti-zionist and anti-Israeli propaganda.

It is important to remember that there was a remarkable and vibrant interfusion of cultural life between Ukrainians and Jews over a long period of time.[51] The first writer who wrote in Hebrew in this area was the Kievan Rabbi Moses Haboleh (1448—1529) and he was succeeded by many talmudic scholars. During the Cossack uprising in the 17th Century many Jewish scholars left Ukraine and settled in Holland and other Western European Countries.

While Yiddish remained the language of common use during this period Hebrew was maintained as the language of prayer. The renaissance of Hebrew and its adaptation to modern life was inspired by the Kievan Jew Achad Haam (1856—1927).

---

[49] "Postanovy Druhoho Velykoho Zboru OUN", Article 17 of "Political Resolutions", in *OUN v Svitli Postanov Velykykh Zboriv*, Munich, 1955, p. 36.

[50] "Postanovy III-ho Nadzvychainoho Velykoho Zboru OUN" in *Ibid.*, pp. 90—103, or in English translation, P. J. Potichnyj and Ye. Shtendera, eds., *Political Thought of the Ukrainian Underground* (forthcoming).

[51] *Entsyklopediia Ukrainoznavstva, op. cit.*, p. 674.

The individual who is commonly regarded as the founder of the Yiddish literary tradition was Shmul Rabinovich more commonly known as Sholom Aleichem who lived in Ukraine from 1859—1916 and by N. Birnbaum from Bukovina. Jewish literature flourished in the late 19th and early 20th centuries. It is important to note that among many Jewish writers writing in Yiddish one finds the presence of certain Ukrainian themes, these writers include Mendele Moicher-Sforim, Sholom Aleichem, Sholom Ash, Sholom Frug, B. Horowitz, M. Olifovich, Sh. Bikel, Rachel Korn. A major segment of these Yiddish writers emigrated from Ukraine mainly to North America during the first three decades of this century. The remnants of the Yiddish school were liquidated in 1950—1952 during Stalin's attack on "cosmopolitanism". A number of major Yiddish institutions were transferred from Ukraine to North America such as theater groups, etc.

Many Jews made major contributions to Ukrainian culture in Ukrainian during the same period. Among the best known Ukrainian poets are L. Pervomaiskyi, S. Holovanivskyi, I. Kulyk, A. Komshtein, A. Katsnelson, R. Troianker. Among the best prose writers and literary critics are: N. Rybak, L. Smilanskyi, V. Toryn, L. Iukhvid (playwright), A. Leites, S. Shchupak, I. Stebun (Katsnelson), L. Iurovska, O. Borshchakivskyi, Ye. Adelheim, A. Hosenpud, J. Hermaize, O. Kurylo, etc. One of the most significant publishers of the Ukrainian language books in the early part of this century was Ia. Orenstein, founder and owner of the "Ukrainian Press" in Kolomyia and Berlin.

JEWISH-UKRAINIAN RELATIONS: THE UKRAINIAN PERSPECTIVE

In approaching this topic, one must introduce a very critical caveat. There is no single "Ukrainian" perspective on Jews. We can exclude the idea that the Ukrainian perspective on the Jew is defined by the "idols of the tribe". We do not believe that Ukrainians as a "tribe" or "race of men" share a genetic perspective on Jews. Clearly, we do not subscribe to the view that part of the Ukrainian "national character" implies a specific and singular perspective on the Jews. We do think that individual Ukrainians do succumb to the "idols of the cave", that is, some individuals have a specific perspective or "cave or den of their own", from which they view the Jews and develop certain characterizations of Jews.

We also believe that a central part of the Ukrainian perspective is derived from what Bacon calls the "idols of the market place", that is images and perceptions "formed by the intercourse and association of men with each other... on account of the commerce and consort of men there". The long intercourse of Ukrainians and Jews in the Central-Eastern part of Europe extending back for over twenty centuries has affected the way in which Ukrainians comprehend Jews. Further a significant part of this perspective are the "idols of the theatre", that is images and perceptions "which have immigrated into men's minds from the various dogmas of philosophies... all the received systems are but so many stage plays, representing worlds of their own creation offer an unreal and scenic fashion."

When we speak of the Ukrainian perspective we recognize that to the person or persons who succumb to these various *Idola,* the content of these perceptions may have positive or negative affect. At this stage we do not think it necessary or useful ourselves to pass any judgement on these *Idola.* Our primary task is to identify and characterize these *Idola* so that we can understand the Ukrainian perspective on the Jews.

The great 16th century humanist Erasmus stated: "if to hate the Jews is to be a good Christian, then we are all good Christians".[52] It is unlikely that this view was entirely foreign to Ukrainians at least since their conversion to Christianity. It is worth remembering, however, that Christianity from its Greek Orthodox origin was imposed as a state religion upon the Rus'-Ukraine population in the 10th century. In the lands of Ukraine, there was never a fervent crusading Christianity which was so characteristic of Western Europe or even Hungary. Christianity in Ukraine was never a proseletyzing force. Indeed, Ukraine itself was a battleground between Polish Catholicism, Greek-Orthodox Christianity and Muscovite Orthodoxy. This struggle between Western (Latin) and Russian Christianity persists to this very day.

Ukraine was also a religious battleground in another sense. From the 13th to the end of the 18th centuries there was the persistent problem of a marauding and expanding Islamic influence emanating from the Ottoman Empire. Ukrainian folklore is full of references to this problem.

It is undeniable that a part of the Ukrainian sensibility towards the Jews relates back to the way in which Christianity in general views the Jews. This attitude, in our view, is fundamentally paradoxical in that Christianity recognizes its links to Jews and Judaism but at the same time views Jews as "recalcitrant aliens" in a Christian environment. This has affected in a substantial manner the way in which Ukrainians have reacted to the presence of Jewish communities in Ukraine, for centuries.

A fascinating example is the Beilis trial where the Tsarist regime attempted to provoke anti-Jewish sentiments in Ukraine and thus drive a wedge between the two communities. It was able to do so successfully by involving the fundamental sentiments in Christianity which view Jews as "recalcitrant aliens" and by playing on the basic ignorance of the masses with regard to Jewish religion and religious ritual. Although the jury of Ukrainian peasants found Beilis innocent the trial itself legitimized and perpetuated the perception of the Jew as a threatening figure in the minds of the people.

The Jew as a paradoxical figure in the Ukrainian perspective is worth exploring further. We have already touched upon the Ukrainian perspective of the

---

[52] Leon Poliakov, "European Anti-semitism East and West", *Commentary,* June 23, 1957, pp. 553—560.

Jew as associated with powerful though foreign forces. However, there is also the Ukrainian perspective of the Jew as "weakling", a pathetic figure who can be swayed and pushed from side to side. For example, in the *VERTEP*, the Jew is portrayed as a relatively insignificant tradesman or obsequious innkeeper who would be willing to provide services to whomever at a small fee.

The image of the Jew in the Ukrainian perspective also has the paradoxical quality of being both "money grubbing" and at the same time "spiritually oriented". This paradoxical view obviously has some bases in fact, for, indeed, the Jew because of economic necessity in Eastern Europe found himself not as a producer but as a middle man in the economic structure of societies. The Jew truly had to survive by his wits and to many people the most important attribute of the Jew was his cunning. At the same time there is the image of the Jews as the "people of the book", or "Knyzhnyky". And it is worth remembering that the spiritual leader of the Jewish community i.e. the Rabbi was looked upon as a very wise man, worthy of great respect.

The late 19th century marks the evolution of some new perspectives of the Jew by the Ukrainians. Three significant factors emerge as powerful forces affecting the relationship between Jews and Ukrainians. These factors emerge from within the Ukrainian community and were efforts at reforming and altering Ukrainian socialization experiences, the economic bases of life and Ukrainian behaviour patterns.

The first factor was the enlightment movement (in Austria-Hungary, the "Prosvita"). There was an effort to develop a more enlightened and better educated Ukrainian public. The vehicles for this effort were a revived school system, the development of community based libraries, newspapers, public information on practical matters, lectures, public performance, etc. The intent of this movement was to raise the literary level of the population and to embed public education into the region.

The second factor was an effort at reforming the economic base of the rural peasantry. This was the development of the "cooperative movement". The intent of the movement was to provide a more secure economic base for the peasantry so that they would not lapse into debt and into the control of the small-town money lender. The traditional pattern was that these money lenders were Jews, Poles and other non-Ukrainians.

The third factor was the development of the anti-alcoholism movement or "Vidrodzhennia". A concerted effort was made to ensure that the Ukrainian peasantry did not spend its time or its disposable income in "Korchma". These inns were traditionally in the hands of Jews.

Although these three forces were not aimed at the Jews in particular, they did have a powerful impact upon the traditional economic viability of many Jews in the villages and small towns in Ukraine.

These factors became intertwined with the spread of industrialization throughout the region in the late 19th and early 20th century. The effect was the growing pauperization and proletarianization of the Jew. In Eastern Europe, this period coincides with the growth of social activism and revolutionary trends among the Jews. This period coincides with the emergence of the Bund and Zionism as two powerful active elements influential on the Jewish community. The Jew became identified as a significant revolutionary element bent on social reform.

It is worth noting that at least one writer, Ivan Franko, portrayed the Jew through a series of literary works in different and paradoxical manners. In *Boa Constrictor* and *Boryslav Smietsia* the protagonists are Jews portrayed as wealthy and oppressive capitalists but in *Surka* Franko describes with great sympathy the life of a poor impoverished Jewess. Franko's most powerful portrait of the Jew is found in his long, narrative poem entitled *Moses*. The Jew Moses becomes the symbol to be emulated by Ukrainians in their search for emancipation and independent homeland. The irony of the story is that Moses never reaches the promised land!

In one of the most remarkable short stories that Franko wrote entitled *Do Svitla*, a small, orphaned, Jewish boy is cast into prison. The story relates how he was taught to read in the prison. The child is shot by a prison guard as he stood next to the cell window with a book in his hand for not observing prison regulations. Franko is an invaluble source of Ukrainian perceptions of the Jew. It is through his work that we get the authentic portrait of the Jew in the social and economic environment of the late 19th and early 20th century in Ukraine.

As far as we are able to ascertain, there does exist only one study of the Jew as he appears in Ukrainian literature. If we are to unearth the real sources of the Ukrainian perception of the Jew, these kinds of studies are indispensable.[53]

The involvement of the Jews in movements of social reform and revolutionary activity in the late 19th and through the early part of the 20th century has had a profound effect on the way in which Ukrainians perceive the Jews. We have identified a series of historical perceptions of Jews by Ukrainians. The 20th century experience of the Jews and their involvement in Western and Eastern European history has created an alternative set of perceptions. What are they? Can we identify the salient features of these perceptions?

By the late 19th century, there was a general awareness that Jews were important figures in movements of social change. Leonard Schapiro in "The Role of the Jews in the Russian Revolutionary Movement", recounts a discussion between Count Witte, then Minister of Finance and Theodore Herzl when the latter visited the Russian Empire in the late summer of 1903. "Witte, duly pointed out to Herzl that while the Jews formed only seven million out of a total popula-

---

[53] The Jewish themes in Ukrainian literature in addition to I. Franko are to be found in the works of T. Shevchenko, N. Gogol, L. Ukrainka, S. Rudanskyj, Ia. Shchoholiv, I. Tohobochnyi, T. Borulliak, Zh. M. Levytskyi, M. Kotsiubynskyi, V. Vynnychenko, O. Oles, A. Liubchenko, L. Pervomaiskyi, M. Khvyliovyi, B. Antonenko-Davydovych, Ia. Hrymailo, Iu. Smolych, P. Myrnyi, I. Kaczurowskyj and others.

tion of 136 million, about fifty per cent of the membership of the revolutionary parties was Jewish. Herzl then asked him whose fault this was. Witte replied: 'I think it is the fault of our government. The Jews are too oppressed.' ... Witte was honest enough in his belief that the Russian government policy of maintaining a large section of the population of the country in permanent subjection was disastrous..."[54]

Obviously, the highest echelons of Tsarist government were fully aware of Jewish involvement in these revolutionary movements. Moreover, the Tsarist police attempted to use this fact by identifying revolutionaries with Jews and to arouse anti-Jewish feelings among the population in the Empire in order to combat the growth of these revolutionary movements. Perhaps their most important efforts was the spreading of the "Protocols of the Elders of Zion".

Ukrainian intellectuals in the same period who were engaged in the organization of their own political movements were not only aware of the activities of these revolutionary Jews, but also had various contacts with them.

This perception of the Jew has become very significant in the minds of many Ukrainian intellectuals and others and persists until today. And this perception is on the whole a very positive one!

However, there is also a perception of the revolutionary Jew as being seduced over time by the bureaucratization of the original Russian revolution.

> "By the time the Bolsheviks seized power, Jewish participation at the highest level of the Party was far from insignificant. Five of the twenty-one full members of the Central Committee were Jews — among the Trotsky and Sverdlov, the real master of the small, but vital, secretarial apparatus of the Party... but Jews abounded at the lower levels of the Party machinery — especially, in the Cheka, and its successors the GPU, OGPU and the NKVD... It is difficult to suggest a satisfactory reason for the prevalence of the Jews in the Cheka. It may be that having suffered at the hands of the former Russian authorities they wanted to seize the reins of real power in the new state for themselves."[55]

In the Ukrainian perspective, the fact that Jews were a significant part of the new Russian state and agents of Russian imperial power, once again, recalled and reinforced the historical perception of the Jew we noted earlier.

Another vital perception of the Jew by the Ukrainians in the early part of the 20th century is that the Jews, as a people, are involved in the struggle for emancipation, and liberation. In intellectual circles, among Ukrainians, there was a sympathetic perception of the Bund and the rise of Zionism. It is historically significant that the Ukrainian Central Rada in 1917 accorded the Jews a significant degree of national autonomy. Examples of the extent to which there was

---

[54] Leonard Schapiro, "The Role of the Jews in the Russian Revolutionary Movement", *The Slavonic and East European Review*, 40, 1961—1962, p. 148.
[55] *Ibid.*, pp. 164—165.

a deep sympathy by the Rada for the aspirations of Jewish national autonomy are found, first, in the fact that a Jewish Ministry of Government was created, second, that full representation for the Jews was ensured in the Rada, third, that Yiddish was recognized as an official language and that all proclamations of government were published also in Yiddish, fourth, that Ukrainian currency even had Yiddish inscribed.[56]

While there was a continuing sympathetic perception of the Jews' aspirations towards national emancipation there was as well the persistent recognition of the Jew as "losers". An important statement of this perception is found in the Resolutions of the Third Extraordinary Grand Assembly of the OUN of August 1943, where it states: "that Ukrainians will not allow themselves to be led to a slaughter in the manner of Jews".[57]

There is a "package" of perceptions by Ukrainians of the Jew which are most relevant in the recent and contemporary periods which are worth exploring. This package one might label as the Jew as examplary. Let us explore this in more detail.

The coming into existence of the State of Israel and the struggle to achieve a Jewish homeland has had a significant impact on the way in which Ukrainians perceive Jews. Among modern states the creation of the State of Israel is unique.

The creation of the State of Israel has a number of exemplary features for the Ukrainians. The creation of the State was the culmination of a long struggle both among the Jews and within the international arena.

The Ukrainians view with fascination the ability of a people to keep the idea of a return to their homeland alive for over 2,000 years. This commitment to the ideal of a "Promised Land" has had a profound impact on the Ukrainians. Moreover, they have witnessed the Jewish ability to conceive of a condition of "Diaspora" as a temporary — even though extended — condition.

Second, Ukrainians watch with considerable interest the way in which Zionism in the late 19th and 20th centuries was able to create a mass movement devoted to the achievement of a political end, namely, the achievement of statehood. Involved in this is a concern and recognition of the importance of organization, commitment, perseverance, and sacrifice in order to achieve the ideal.

Third, Ukrainians recognized in Zionism that it is possible to overcome divisions and discord among groups within a people and to achieve solidarity through the commitment to a political objective — statehood.

Fourth, Ukrainians observed the way in which Zionism, as a political movement, was able to operate and to achieve legitimacy within the international arena. There is a recognition that the struggle for statehood must take place indigenously within a people and externally by enlisting support, exerting pressure and making representations internationally.

---

[56] Solomon I. Goldelman, *op. cit.*
[57] "Postanovy III-ho...", *op. cit.*, pp. 90—103.

Perhaps the most profound impact that Zionism and the creation of the State of Israel has had on Ukrainian perception of the Jews involves the notion of struggle as a necessary prelude to success. Any achievement of national liberation and statehood can only come about after a prolonged period of suffering, organized struggle, and even the necessity of armed struggle.

To the Ukrainian mind there are many intriguing similarities between the history of Zionism in the 19th and 20th century and the Ukrainian struggle for national independence. The parallels are fascinating.

First there was the creation of the political movement in the 19th century dedicated to the achievement of independence. Then there was the attempt at statehood during 1917—1920 which ended disastrously. This resulted in the establishment of a more militant organization which led to an armed struggle during World War II. This again ended in failure and the imposition of foreign domination over Ukraine. The "idea" of statehood is sustained most militantly among Ukrainians in the diaspora. Among the Diaspora Ukrainians, efforts such as the World Congress of Free Ukrainians and other organizations sustain the ideal of statehood. As well, these organizations attempt to use the international arena as a platform to achieve their political objectives.

While the struggle occurs within the Ukrainian diaspora, a different struggle takes place within Ukraine. Under conditions of foreign domination the struggle focuses on issues such as individual rights, human rights, national rights, free cultural expressions, resistance to Russification. In effect the visible expression of the struggle from the outside is the character and quality of dissent within the USSR.

This condition has led to the creation of a *de facto* common front among Jews and Ukrainians within the USSR. We have ample evidence of the ongoing collaboration and solidarity between Jews and Ukrainians in their struggle for individual and cultural rights over the past twenty years. We have the personal testimony of Moroz, Suslensky, Karavanskyi and other former Ukrainians and Jewish prisoners. A crucial document which attests to this collaboration is Dzyuba's speech at Babi Yar.[58]

It is worth noting that the Soviets have recognized the development of this common front between Jews and Ukrainians within Ukraine. They have reacted by publishing provocative material which portrays the Jews and Ukrainian nationalists as Nazis and they have condemned Zionists as Nazi collaborators.[59]

The Ukrainian community in their diaspora has tried to develop a parallel

---

[58] Ivan Dzyuba, "Vystup u Babynomu Iaru" (29 September 1966) in V. Chornovil, *Lykho z Rozumu*, Paris, 1967, pp. 303—308. See also "Interview with Heifetz: A View from the Inside", *The Ukrainian Weekly*, February 1, 1981, pp. 7, 10. A rather interesting statement can be found in "Aid to Ukrainian Jewry" in "The Frontiers of Culture", published in English translation in *ABN Correspondence*, Vol. 33, No. 1, 1982, pp. 24—26.

[59] See for example Kichko's, *Iudaizm bez prykras*. Kiev, 1963 or V. Iu. Ievdokymenko and V. O. Ihnatov, *op. cit.*, Kiev, 1981.

common front between themselves and Jews in their diaspora. Indeed, the efforts at developing a Jewish-Ukrainian dialogue have come predominantly from the Ukrainian community. They are attempting to create a condition of mutual understanding between Jews and Ukrainians and they are trying to use the example of Jewish-Ukrainian collaboration within Ukraine as a viable and significant example.

JEWISH-UKRAINIAN RELATIONS: THE JEWISH PERSPECTIVE

It is significant that the *Jewish Encyclopaedia* does not have a separate entry for Ukraine. The discussion of Jewish history which is located in the region of Ukraine occurs in the Encyclopaedia under Russia, Poland or Austria-Hungary. It would appear that the notion of a distinctive Ukrainian culture or Ukrainian nation state is absent from those who compiled the *Jewish Encyclopaedia*.

This observation may very well betray a most important feature in our efforts to approach the question of Jewish-Ukrainian relations. For it is the authority of the *Encyclopaedia* itself which drives one to conceive of Jewish history in the Ukrainian region not as a distinctive, separate and identifiable history, but rather as a part of a larger history, namely Polish or Russian history.

This portrait of Jewish history is confirmed by many sources including Moses A. Shulvass in his book *Jewish Culture in Eastern Europe: The Classical Period*.[60] Shulvass argues that there are two historical periods of Jewish presence in the region called Ukraine. The first period runs from 1st Century A.D. until 13th Century A.D. As we have discovered earlier, these were Jewish settlements in the Crimea and the Black Sea area very early on. Under the influence of the Khazar people and their conversion to Judaism in the 8th century, Jewish settlements flourished and influence expanded. "It seems that Southern Ukraine's Jewish population together with the remnants of the Jewish Khazarians, were obliterated by the terrible invasions of the Tatars during the first half of the thirteenth century. In the decades following the Tatar invasions no Jewish settlements are known to have existed in the Ukraine."[61]

The second significant period of Jewish history in Ukraine coincides with the extension of Polish rule in Ukraine. The Jewish perspective on the character and quality of Jewish life in historic Poland on the whole is very positive. By the end of the 14th century the Polish Kingdom extended from the Baltic to the Black Sea. Poland was a major trading force and a major supplier of agricultural products to Western Europe.

As a result of the crusades, anti-Jewish legislation "and the repeated blood

---

[60] Moses A. Shulvass, *Jewish Culture in Eastern Europe: The Classical Period*, New York, KTAV Publishing, 1975.

[61] *Ibid.*, pp. 1—2.

accusations, followed by bloody pogroms",[62] there was a mass emigration of Jews from Germany into the Polish Kingdom. And on the whole Jews were able to establish a viable life in this territory. "In 1264 Duke Boleslaw of Kalisz granted them [the Jews] a charter which became the legal foundation for their settlement. This charter, modeled after a constitution granted the Jews a few decades earlier in Austria and in Bohemia, was quite favourable to them. It became the Magna Charta of Medieval Polish Jewry.[63] These rights were later on extended to all Jews in the Polish Kingdom by Casimir the Great (1333—1370).

Jewish prosperity in the Polish Kingdom is well documented by Dubnow and others. It is interesting to note that the size of the Jewish population in the Polish Kingdom is estimated to have been between 70,000 and 100,000 in the year 1550. In the year 1648 the population is estimated to have been between 300,000 to 500,000 which would have made it the largest territorial concentration of Jews in the world.

Shulvass argues that as Polish dominance over the Ukrainian area developed in the 16th and 17th centuries, the Jews benefitted tremendously. "In the then newly colonized areas of the Ukraine, the main occupation of the Jews was the forming of tolls and taxes and leasing of estates. They became a well-to-do class. Most of the Jewish sections in the cities had beautiful stone houses; wealthy men built beautiful synagogues, often designed by famous architects. The Jewish section in many cities and towns expanded considerably in area... The growth of the Jewish population, its economic success and the influence which Jewish magnates exerted in the royal court..."[64] best defines the depth of the prosperity of the Jews in the Polish Kingdom.

We have already indicated the manner in which Ukrainians in this very same period perceived the Jew as appendages to their domination by the foreign Polish nobility. We can see from the above that there was a clear class and economic division between the Jew and the indigenous Ukrainian population. There was also a further religious element which complicated the relationship between the Ukrainians, the Poles and the Jews.

> "Enormous estates and numerous villages, inhabited by Ukrainian peasants, were in the hands of wealthy Polish magnates, who utilized all the rights of feudal lords. The peasant-serfs or *Khlopi*, were alien to their masters, both in religion and nationality. In the eyes of the Catholics, particularly the clergy, the Greek-Orthodox faith was the religion of the *Khlopi*. There was an attempt to uproot it through an improved Church union. The Poles regarded the Russians and Ukrainians as a lowly race, one that was more Asiatic than European... The Polish Magnates usually lived at some distance

---

[62] *Ibid.*, p. 3. [63] *Ibid.*, p. 4.
[64] *Ibid.*, p. 9.

from their Ukrainian estates; so their possessions were administered by lessees and bookkeepers. The village lessees included many Jews... Jews acquired leases on inns, on the distilling and sale of liquor, dairies, flower mills, and occasionally also on tax farming on behalf of the landed gentry. Along with the lease the Jews inherited from the landed gentry some of the rights over the serfs. The lessees endeavored to extract as much revenue as possible from the nobleman's estates, and to do that it was necessary to exploit the peasantry."[65]

While the Jew found himself in an enviable and successful economic situation in the Polish dominated Ukraine, there were the seeds of deep antagonisms in place. These antagonisms resulted in perhaps the most significant event in Ukrainian history which had a catastrophic effect on Jewish perception of Ukrainians. Once again Dubnov best summarizes this:

"The contempt on the part of the gentry and the Catholic clergy for the party of the *Khlopi* and the attempts to Catholicize the Greek Orthodox Ukrainians by way of the Church Union, colored the economic antagonism with a religious hue. The subjugated peasantry always grumbled angrily; and from time to time agrarian disorders erupted in various localities. The Ukrainian peasant detested the Polish *pan*, the nobleman, the Catholic, the Pole, the [LIAKH]. But he hated even more the Jewish lessee — the gentry's supervisor, the alien, the 'un-Christian'. The Jew thus found himself between the hammer and the anvil: between the landed gentry and the *Khlopi*, between the Catholic and the Greek-Orthodox Church, between the Pole and the Ukrainian. Three classes, three religions, three nationalities clashed on a foundation in whose depths volcanig forces lay dormant; and the explosion was inevitable."[66]

This explosion occurred in 1648 with the Khmelnytskyi uprising. In the annals of Jewish history the Khmelnytskyi period is known as the Great Catastrophe or as the *Gzerah!* This period is recognized as having a status equivalent to the Holocaust of the Second World War. The Jews at that period suffered immensely. "When the people went on a rampage, the Jew suffered more than the nobleman. And it is not the Jewish lessees who suffered, but the entire Jewish communities, which had no relation to the leasehold. A new ominous and sinister force — the Ukrainian *Haidamak* — burst forth into Jewish history. It leaves in its wake a deep bloody trace, which can be seen and recognized during the course of three centuries."[67]

---

[65] Simon Dubnov, *History of the Jews: From Cromwell's Commonwealth to the Napoleonic Era*, New York, Thomas Yoselaff, 1971, Vol. IV, p. 26.
[66] *Ibid.*, pp. 26—27.
[67] *Ibid.*, p. 29. See also Abraham Berger (Review of *The Fatal Events of 1648*, Wilno, Yiddish Scientific Institute, 1938) in *Jewish Social Studies*, 2 April 1940, pp. 217—218.

It is estimated that "Ukrainian Kozaks under the leadership of Bohdan Khmelnytskyi are said to have massacred between 100,000 and 250,000 Jews." While these figures are often the subject of dispute, it is, nevertheless, obvious that in view of the total estimated Jewish population of that time of between 300,000 and 500,000, the scale of the slaughter was enormous.

There is no doubt that 1648 is a traumatic date in Jewish-Ukrainian history. We have seen how, quoting Dubnov, the Jews found themselves trapped as third parties and the major victims in a Ukrainian-Polish conflict.

There is, however, a further significant insight of the way in which Jewish perceptions of Ukrainians were molded and it is certainly worth explaining. The Jews emigrated into the Ukrainian territories in the 15th and 16th centuries as appendages of the Polish Kingdom. We have seen how the Poles viewed Ukrainians with contempt and with a high degree of disdain. This same perception of the Ukrainians as "peasants", "lower christians", and in general as marginally civilized was transmitted to the Jews and formed the basis of their perceptions. Their view is best articulated by Shulvass when he states:

> "The Ukraine was a frontier country, and the Jews who settled there were true pioneers who brought material and spiritual culture with them. Economic opportunity was virtually unlimited. Constituting the most civilized part of the population of this wild and waste land, they cooperated closely with the Polish landlords who developed the country, and were an important factor in the tremendous effort to colonize it. Their main occupation was in the area of management. They were the leading farmers of customs and other categories of taxation; they rented distilleries, breweries, inns, and similar enterprises. And as the opportunities were great, the wave of Jews going to the Ukraine persisted uninterrupted until the year of the Great Catastrophe."[68]

What is revealing about this quotation is not the characterization of the Jews' economic position in Ukraine — there seems to be the consensus among historians both Jewish and Ukrainians on this subject — but rather the portrait of the Jew as the transmitter and bearer of civilization and "material and spiritual culture" into a "wild and wasteland". To us this view betrays a fundamental perception or, in Baconian language, one of the idols of the theatre and the market place which has persisted through the course of four centuries of Jewish-Ukrainian relations. How can we articulate it?

Among Jews, and others as well, there is the view that Jews play a unique role in world history. It is the Jew who bears the responsibility of bringing spiritual values and the concerns with culture and civilization to a world which

---

This composite work consists of a report of W. Latzki-Bertoldi's Yiddish translation of the famous contemporary chronicle of the Khmelnytskyi revolt, *Yewen Metsulah* by Nathan Nata Hanover.

[68] M. A. Shulvass, *op. cit.*, p. 10.

at times is overwhelmingly materialistic, anti-intellectual or hedonistic. This conception of the role of the Jew in alien cultures has deeply affected the way in which the Jew relates to and perceives other cultures. Shulvass' statements that the Jews were the carriers of civilization to a peasant region, in a deep sense, identify this historic perception of the role of the Jew among the gentiles. There is a significance, though often not articulated, and truth to Shulvass' statements. We can go even further. The identification of the Ukrainians as peasants, semi-asiatics, perhaps even uncivilized has had a profound impact on the way in which the Jews perceive Ukrainians. This portrait of the Ukrainians as being one small step away from barbarism is a theme found in Yiddish literature.[69] It is therefore not surprising to the Jewish mentality that Ukrainians are prone to lapse into a condition of barbarism and to vent their animosity, frustration and anger against the Jews as the carriers of civilization. This is the reason for so many Jews the name Ukrainian conjures up a fascinating package of images — peasant, drunkard, barbarian, a creature prone to excess and lacking both culture and civility, a fierce, threatening figure when he is angered or given to his passions. This package of images also helps explain why, to the Jewish perception, the Ukrainian is the symbolic embodiment of the authentic anti-semite. The reason for this is that the authentic anti-semite is the open enemy of the Jew who acts as the symbol of spirituality and civilization.

The historical legacy emanating from the Khmelnytskyi era cannot be underestimated in terms of its effect on the Jewish perception of the Ukrainian. In the Jewish view, the Khmelnytskyi uprising has little significance as a struggle for national emancipation. Its significance lies in the fact that it portrays the historic and tragic condition of the Jew in a gentile world.[70] The lesson to be drawn from this period is that the Jew, in spite of everything, ends up being the victim in any struggles between opposing nations or ethnic groups. The Jew is always caught in the middle. He is always the sacrificial lamb when historic forces come into conflict.

The subsequent reading of the Jewish presence in Ukraine is rather simple. There are periods of relative calm when Jews living among some measure of economic prosperity. These periods, however, are shattered by "volcanic uprisings", (to use Dubnov's phrase), pogroms and outbreaks of violent anti-semitism. Possony, for example, relates this cycle of peace and tranquility followed by turmoil and violence.[71] The periods of turmoil are 1648—1654, 1760—1778, 1918—1921, and 1941—1945.

---

[69] See for example Edward Alexander, "The Destruction and Resurrection of the Jews in the Fiction of I. B. Singer", *Judaism*, 25, Winter 1976, pp. 98—106.

[70] See for example M. Agursky, "Ukrainian Nationalism Poses Threat to Jews Again", *Jerusalem Post*, March 7, 1977. The author is a prominent scholar and a recent emigrant from the USSR.

[71] Stefan T. Possony, "The Ukrainian-Jewish Problem: Historical Retrospective", *op. cit.*

There are two ways to understand this cycle. The first is to identify these periods with the struggle for Ukrainian emancipation and autonomy. The second is to identify these periods with the victimization of the Jews caught in historic struggles in which they had no vested interest. What remains constant in the Jewish reading of the Ukrainian history is that the periods of turmoil are associated with the outbreak of this authentic anti-semitism. The Jewish perception of Ukrainian history, therefore, reads as a continuous reverberation of a single theme. When Ukrainians take up the struggle against whatever foreign oppressor, this struggle results in the persecution of Jews.

There has been a significant literature which delves into Jewish-Ukrainian relations during these periods of struggle. We have pointed to some of it previously.[72] What is indisputable in reviewing this literature is that the Jewish perception of these periods of intense turmoil revolves around a preoccupation with the victimization of the Jew.

We have identified one of the persistent themes in the interpretation of Jewish history in terms of the conflict between spirituality and barbarism or between civilization and culture as opposed to hedonism and anti-intellectuality. The consequence of this is the historic tragedy of the Jew as victim.

There is a further variation of this theme which is worth exploring. Isaac Deutscher in *The Non-Jewish Jew and Other Essays* argues that in a socio-economic and, more importantly, in a psychological sense the Jew has always been a marginal figure in a Gentile world.[73] This situation has defined the perception and outlook of the Jew in relation to the world around him. It is this situation of marginality which has enabled the Jew to assume the role of the critic of dominant cultures. As Deutscher states "they were *a priori* exceptional in that as Jews they dwelt on the borderlines of various civilizations, religions, and national cultures. They were born and brought up on the borderline of various epochs. Their mind matured where the most diverse cultural influences crossed and fertilized each other. They lived on the margins or in the nooks and crannies of their respective nations. Each of them was in society and yet not in it, of it and yet not of it. It was this that enabled them to rise in thought above their societies, above their nations, above their times and generations, and to strike out mentally into wide new horizons and far into the future."[74] While this characterization is aimed at exploring the presence of Jewish intellectuals in societies, we think Deutscher's point is valid in exploring the psychological as well as socio-economic situation of Jews in general in a Gentile world. This helps explain, indeed, the inability or the failure of Jews or Jewish movements to become deeply entwined in movements of national liberation. But while this is true, Jews and Jewish movements have had major

---

[72] See footnotes, 6, 10, 19, 22, 24, 36, 65, and 67.
[73] Isaac Deutscher, *The Non-Jewish Jew and Other Essays*, London, Oxford University Press, 1968.
[74] *Ibid.*, p. 27.

roles to play in movements of social reform. This may explain why Jews, on the whole, had no involvement with Ukrainian movements of national liberation (1648, 1917—1920), while Jews had a deep involvement in the Russian revolution whose goals were primarily social reform.

There is another interesting variation on these same ideas proposed by Albert Memmi in *Portrait of a Jew:*

> "I believe, in short that there is a Jewish fate, a specific Jewish fate. This fate makes the Jew a minority being; different; separated both from himself and from others; a being abused in his culture and in his history, in his past and in his daily life — in the end an abstract being...
>
> ...Yes, as a Jew, I am above all an oppressed person and the Jewish fate is essentially a condition of oppression...
>
> ...As a Jew I am a man of deficiencies. Those deficiencies are actual defects in my existence; I am not only suspected and accused, I am bullied, restricted, curtailed in my daily life, in my development as a man. These objective deficiencies, often institutional, involve true restrictions, even serious destruction of the soul of the Jew. For the most serious element, perhaps, the one most difficult to admit, is that the Jewish fate is a degrading fate...
>
> ...The sad reality, unfortunately, is that all oppression debases and ruins the oppressed. Our weak reaction to oppression, for example, and our resignation before catastrophe are not a sign of a certain obscure metaphysical grandure, or the proof of an intransigent moral will, as we like to say. They are the symptoms of a terrible usury of an accumulated historical lassitude."[75]

To most Jews, the portrait that Memmi draws would be fairly accurate. The Jew in his perception of his relations to Ukrainians or almost any other national group could and would point to situations of oppression. The explanation of that oppression might be economic, sociological or whatever, or it may be based upon the view that the Gentile world is fundamentally anti-semitic. As well, it appears that Memmi's association of the condition of oppression with catastrophies is also very appropriate for the Jewish perception of Jewish history and the Jewish fate in Ukraine as well as other countries.

The cycle of tranquility and prosperity followed by upheaval and catastrophe is one of the central premises of the Jewish reading of their own history and the relation between their own history and the history of other nations. It is therefore not surprising that the Jewish portrait of Jewish-Ukrainian relations follows along this cycle.

Simon Dubnov in his *History of the Jews,* Vol. 4, devotes a major part of the first section of his book to what he calls "the dreadful year of the Ukrain-

---

[75] Albert Memmi, *Portrait of a Jew* (Translated from French by E. Abbot), London, Eyre and Spottiswoode, 1963, 320—321.

ian massacre — the *Gezerah* of 1648." Drawing upon a variety of documentary sources, Dubnov provides us with a picture of devastation and horror. "The losses of Polish Jewry in the years of the horrible massacres from 1648 to 1656 were frightening. The Jewish Chronicles' appraisals of those who perished fluctuate between 100,000, and 500,000 victims. If one were to take an average between these figures, it would also surpass the catastrophies of the crusades and the 'black death' in Western Europe."[76]

One of the consequences of the coming of a catastrophe to the Jewish people is the revival of a yearning for redemption or, the revival of a messianic spirit. In the annals of Jewish history, the catastrophe of 1648 is very closely linked to a rebirth of the messianic movement. This messianic movement gripped Jewish communities throughout Eastern and Central Europe as well as the Ottoman Empire. "...a new messianic movement ripened — the mightiest since the time of BAR Kokhba. It came into being ten years after the Ukrainian-Polish catastrophe in Turkey, which was close to the site of the tribulations. It aroused the entire Jewish world, and left deep traces in the history of the people."[77]

If Ivan Franko's novels encapsulate the quality of the Ukrainian experience in the early part of the 20th century then it would be true to say that Isaac B. Singer's novels do the same for the Jewish experience in the same part of the world.

There are a variety of intertwined themes which permeate the writings of Singer. The first theme is that the environment in which Jews were forced to live their daily lives was hostile, threatening and prone to "volcanic eruptions". The second major theme which emerges from these works is that the Jew is the helpless victim of an environment over which he has no control. While Jewish culture, ritual and experience betrays qualities of humour and even irony, the inevitable fact about Jewish existence is its precarious fate. It is no wonder therefore that the Holocaust has both a dramatic-historical and deeply symbolic meaning in the works of Singer. In *The Family Moskat* Singer concludes with the statement "death is the Messiah. That's the real truth." "Singer sees the major catastrophies of Jewish history in the Diaspora as so many announcements of the Holocaust, of which they are the prototypes. Nowhere in his fiction does Singer assume that the Jews were accidental victims of the Holocaust, or that disaster might just as well have befallen another people... But if Singer avoids the pitfalls of the oppressed which assumes the perfect innocence of the Jews and the accidental nature of their victimization, he may be said to go to the other extreme in that he tends to view the Nazis as only the latest in the long succession of those murderous outsiders who have obtruded themselves upon Jewish history again and again. 'Yes', sighs the narrator of *The Family Moskat*, 'Every generation had its pharaohs and Hamans and Chmielnickis. Now it was Hitler'."[78]

---

[76] Simon Dubnov, *op. cit.*, p. 45.
[77] *Ibid.*, p. 51.
[78] Edward Alexander, *op. cit.*, pp. 98—99.

Singer's preoccupation with catastrophy is worked out in the historical context in his novel *The Slave*. The setting of this novel is the second half of the 17th century after the catastrophy which beset the Jews and associated with Khmelnytskyi Singer poses the perennial Jewish question when they confront disaster — "why did this happen to us?" In the novel answer comes "it was God's will, but why? What sins did the small children commit? They were burned alive... There was a limit to what the human mind could accept. It was beyond the power of any man to contemplate all these attrocities and mourn them adequately... Did the creator require the assistance of Cossacks to reveal this nature?"[79]

The incomprehensibility of the massacres, slaughter or victimization of the Jew in his historical settings through the ages obsessed not only Singer but other Yiddish writers as well. For example Sholom Aleichem responds to this dilemma in terms of irony, humor, and even satire. But the central preoccupation with the Jew as oppressed and on the brink of continuous disaster could be seen as the element of thematic unity throughout all of this literature.

The Holocaust of the Second World War was more than just another instance of the cycle of catastrophies endemic to Jewish history. The scale of the Holocaust, its premediated nature, the implication of so many nations in the destruction of European Jewry, left a profound and lasting effect upon the Jews.

One can indeed say that the Holocaust destroyed totally two conceptions of Jewish survival which seemed to be viable prior to the war. The first was the conception that the Jew had a stake in the major movements of twentieth century enlightenment and movements of social reform. This view had captured the imagination of many Jews and had seemed an adequate response to the plight of the Jew in Europe. Progress of mankind through education, equality, eradication of prejudice, etc., it was believed, would result in the ability of the Jew to exist without being the victim of periodic upheavals.

The second conception was fundamentally religious in character. The Jew had to live a life according to religious tradition which set him outside the mainstream of other cultures. The salvation of the Jew rested upon obeying the will of God and deliverance might arise when the Messiah would come. It is interesting to note that Singer's book *Satan in Goray* ends with the following: "let none attempt to force the Lord; to end our pain within the world: the Messiah will come in God's own time."[80]

Both these conceptions proved inadequate in saving the Jew from the Holocaust in Europe. The remnants of European Jewry which survived the War could find no solace or hope in either of these prescriptions. The Holocaust may have also created a condition where it was no longer feasible or acceptable for Jews willingly to admit that they had a role to play in the history of nations as what Deutscher calls the "outsider" or, to use Memmi's phrase, as the "oppressed".

---

[79] *Ibid.*, pp. 99.
[80] *Ibid.*, p. 103.

The consequence of willingly accepting these roles has always and would always lead to catastrophies. The Holocaust created the condition where Jews no longer accepted the cylce of tranquility followed by catastrophe and they would do all they could to create conditions where a Holocaust would "never again" be possible.

As in the 17th century, the cycle of Holocaust followed by deliverance emerged once again in the mid-20th century, this time the State of Israel emerged from the ashes of the Second World War. This is the single most important fact in understanding the way in which contemporary Jews, understand the world and the way they perceive others.

Zionism is the focus point of any contemporary discussion of the place of Jews in the modern era. If we are to address the question of Jewish-Ukrainian relations in the past World War era, then it is necessary to clarify some of the fundamental qualities of Zionism and its possible impact on Jewish perspectives.

The first and obvious fact resulting from Zionism and its success in creating the State of Israel is that the Jew in the post-war period has been successful. The success in creating a nation state as a homeland for Jews fills most Jews with a deep and abiding sense of pride. This sense of pride is closely related to a further quality which has emerged in the Jewish perspective in the recent period that is a sense of potency.[81] This is radically different from the sense of victimization which we discussed earlier.

The reality of Zionism and the State of Israel has also created a new image of the Jew as builder. The process of founding a nation-state and building it in a variety of meanings, economically, socially, culturally, militarily etc., has deeply affected the self-understanding of the Jew. In terms of the representation of Israel to the world, the Jew as nation-builder is probably most important.

Another way of understanding this same idea is to think of Zionism and the State of Israel as putting to an end the necessity of Jews thinking of themselves as perennial victims or, the "oppressed." Fate now has less of an impact upon the way in which the Jew understands himself, and the Jew as creator of his own fate, as "maker", or "doer", or "builder" has a more powerful reality today.

The consequence of this new image of the Jew has had an effect upon the way in which Jews, both within Israel and outside of Israel relate to other national groups. There is a general feeling within the Jewish community in Israel and in the diaspora that relations between Jews and other national groups must involve the State of Israel. It is almost as if the lead role and the definition of any relationships must be assumed by the Jewish national state. This can be seen in an obvious way in terms of relations between the Jewish community in the United States and the larger American political community. Recently, rela-

---

[81] See for example Solomon Grayzel, *A History of the Contemporary Jews, From 1900 to the Present*, New York, Atheneum, 1972; Robert Chazan and Marc Lee Raphael, *Modern Jewish History: A Source Reader*, New York, Schocken Books, 1974

tions between the State of Israel and the United States have become strained. Consequently, the American Jewish community has become increasingly and openly critical of the American government. This pattern of defining the attitude of Jews within Israel and in the diaspora towards nations and national groups solely in terms of the national interest of the State of Israel has both a positive and negative quality. Positively one can say that at long last Jews can relate to others on an equal basis in terms of some sense of "national interest". This is very important in understanding the way in which Jews want to be understood by others. However, there is the implication in this argument that diaspora Jews must define their perspective in terms of the "national interest" of Israel. In many situations, the common practice of diaspora Jews is to do exactly this. In other circumstances, extending the logic of this position can create some difficulties.

Let us take a current example. It may be that it is in the "national interest" of the State of Israel to ensure that as many Soviet Jews as possible emigrate from the USSR to Israel. Indeed, the general Jewish attitude in the diaspora, as well, has been defined in these terms. Unfortunately, the remaining Jewish population in the USSR may not identify the "national interest" of the State of Israel. What then should be the attitude of Jews towards Soviet Jewry? Or, can one develop an argument which could relate the notion of the "national interest" of Israel to the relations of Jews and Ukrainians in Ukrainian SSR. The reality of Israel makes it increasingly difficult for Jews to develop perspectives on problems independent of some concern with the "national interest" of Israel.

One may be able to define the wellbeing of diaspora Jews independent of the Jewish homeland. However, in terms of the contemporary preoccupations of Jewish communities, it would appear that this is not the case. The wellbeing of diaspora Jewry is totally linked to and dependent upon the Jewish homeland.

This is the context in which Jews today approach the question of Jewish-Ukrainian relations. Fundamentally, if the link between Jewish-Ukrainian relations and the State of Israel cannot be made, then there is little prospect for eliciting any interest from Jews on this question. The fact of the State of Israel is so overpowering a force on the perspectives of contemporary Jewry, that there is relatively little ground for establishing independent concerns, preoccupations, problems etc. on the part of Jews in the diaspora.

We have earlier identified a number of ways in which Jews conceived of themselves prior to the establishment of the State of Israel.[82] The fact remains that there are significant number of Jews in the diaspora who are very unlikely to emigrate to Israel in the immediate future or who, indeed, want to emigrate. The perspective of the Jew that we have identifed earlier remain important

---

[82] See for example Joseph Rothschild, "Ethnic Peripheries Versus Ethnic Cores: Jewish Political Strategies in Interwar Poland", *Political Science Quarterly*, Vol. 96, No. 4, Winter 1981—82, pp. 591—606.

and valuable to them. And, further questions, of their relationships to other national groups or questions revolving around their minority status within a particular nation state need not be mediated or linked to the State of Israel. Stated in other terms, the fate of Soviet Jewry (and not merely their emigration) should be of major concern to everyone but particularly to diaspora Jews.

In this context the problem of Jewish-Ukrainian relations may assume a new importance. Jews should be deeply concerned about the manner in which the remaining Jewish community in Ukraine can survive. Indeed, Ukrainians, as well, should be concerned about the Jewish minority in Ukraine. The question of minority rights touches upon the issue of human rights; these issues are of major concerns both to Jews and Ukrainians. Furthermore the United Nations Declaration of Human Rights argues that the right to culture must be ensured for all nationalities or national groups in all countries. This issue clearly touches directly upon both Jews and Ukrainians. One can argue further that Jews should be deeply concerned about the capacity of Ukrainians to achieve their full independence and emancipation.

CONCLUSION

At the beginning of this paper, we commented on the Canadian dilemma of "two solitudes" and suggested that it would be wise to bear it in mind as we investigate Jewish-Ukrainian relations. Our investigation of Jewish-Ukrainian relations, indeed, substantiates the notion that Jews and Ukrainians, in their relations over a prolonged historical period, live in "two solitudes." Georg Wilhelm Friedrich Hegel in his Introduction to *The Philosophy of History* stated "But what experience and history teach is this—that people and governments never have learned anything from history, or acted on principles deduced from it."[83]

When we examine the fundamental conceptions which underlie the way in which Ukrainians view their history and their relations to Jews and the way in which Jews understand their history and their relations to Ukrainians, it is clear that we are locked in a Gordian knot which appears to be insurmountable. Mere mortals appear to be unable to escape from their own history, to detach themselves from their fundamental perceptions of history and from the "Idola" which confound their minds. If we are to believe Hegel, mortals cannot even learn from history!

And, yet, there does appear to be some significant ways in which Jews and Ukrainians can and should, together, undertake the exploration of their dilemma. One cannot undo or re-do history. James Joyce in *Ulysses* has Stephen claim that "History is a nightmare from which I am trying to awake." However,

---

[83] George Wilhelm Friedrich Hegel in his Introduction to *The Philosophy of History*, New York, 1956, Dover Publications, translated by J. Sibree, p. 6.

there remains a most important intellectual task ahead of us, and that is to unravel the complex nature of the Jewish interpretation of their own history and to see how that interpretation affects the way in which Jews perceive Ukrainians and vice-versa. This is the preliminary task. We must go beyond that, to the more critical problem of transforming those perceptions into bases for mutual understanding and for joint efforts. These efforts revolve around the fact that there remains some 800,000 Jews who still live in Ukraine. It would appear unlikely that this entire population will uproot itself and remove itself from Ukraine. How are these people likely to survive? What kind of attitude should Jews have towards this population? What should be the attitude of Ukrainians towards this population? There is the further problem of what should be the relationship between Jews and Ukrainians outside Ukraine? As we have seen, Jews have had a significant influence upon Ukrainians in their diaspora. The search for an independent homeland for Ukrainians, independent of Soviet domination, is likely to remain a driving force inspiring Ukrainian activity in their diaspora. What should be the Jewish attitude towards these aspirations? Historically, Jews have been deeply involved in the struggles for human rights and national liberation. Is this not a basis for joint efforts between Jews and Ukrainians?

There are a further number of important intellectual efforts of mutual interest which should be undertaken. Yiddish literature is a subject of intense intellectual interest today. That literature, contextually, is strongly rooted in the Jewish historical experience in Ukraine. We have also seen, that there is a significant portrait of Jewish life and Jewish themes in Ukrainian literature. We should devote ourselves to this kind of literary exploration so that we may recognize the important cultural relationship and influence of Jews and Ukrainians in the Yiddish and Ukrainian literary traditions. The intermingling of culture between Jews and Ukrainians extends to the level of folklore and this subject, as well, is an appropriate subject for intellectual work.

While we remain captives of our own history, it does appear to us that the inquiry into Jewish-Ukrainian relations is a most serious concern which raises vital subjects of inquiry and which does have some profound importance for the nature of political action. We have attempted a preliminary investigation into this subject. We have raised some problems, some questions, some serious concerns. Obviously, much work is required in the future.

MODERNIZATION AND ITS IMPACT ON
JEWISH-UKRAINIAN RELATIONS

INTRODUCTION

Our paper entitled "Jewish-Ukrainian Relations: Two Solitudes" had a number of peculiarities. First, it provoked considerable interest in Canada, the United States adn even in Europe.[1] It is clear to us that the question of Jewish-Ukrainian relations, in whatever aspect, is of deep significance for many people and it is a topic long overdue for discussion. Second, we found that there was some advantages in undertaking a discussion of Jewish-Ukrainian relations from Canada. In the paper we argued that there are some intriguing similarities between the relations of Jews and Ukrainians and those of French and English Canadians. The most concise metaphor to characterize French and English Relations in Canada is 'two solitudes.' The relation between Jews and Ukrainians appears to us to be strikingly similar. Third, to our surprise, we found that there is a striking paucity of published material on almost every aspect of Jewish-Ukrainian relations.[2] This is a very fertile and untilled area of scholarly

---

[1] This paper has now been published in the English in *The Ukrainian Weekly* July 18-August 8, 1982, in Germany in *Jahrbuch der Ukrainekunde*, 1982.

[2] The bibilographic difficulties one confronts when approaching this question arises, in part, from the view of many Jewish scholars that Jewish history in the region now called Ukraine was part of a larger imperial history, namely Polish or Russian. The question of Jewish-Polish relations or Jewish-Russian relations, therefore, is much richer in bibliographic resources than Jewish-Ukrainian relations. An example can be found in Ellis Rivkin, *The Shaping of Jewish History: A Radical New Interpretation*, N.Y., Scribner's Sons, 1971. A further example is found in Jonathan Charles Frankel, *Prophecy and Policies: Socialism, Nationalism and the Russian Jews*, 1862-1927, Cambridge, Cambridge University Press, 1981.

investigations and research. Fourth, we also discovered that there appears to be some reluctance on the part of a variety of people to entertain seriously, thoughtfully and dispassionately, the subject of Jewish-Ukrainian relations. Most historical questions, especially if the history is a tragic one, provoke passion, involvement, concern. It is only human to find it difficult to distance oneself from historical tragedy, especially if one's own history is linked to that tragedy. In approaching the question of Jewish-Ukrainian relations, we must be deeply sensitive to this problem. And yet, we should not shy away from difficult questions and problems.[3]

THE LEGACY OF HISTORY

James Joyce in *Ulyssess* has stephen Daedalus claim that "History is a nightmare from which I am trying to awake." There is no doubt that, both for Jews and Ukrainians, history has nightmarish qualities. Moreover, when you cross-breed these nightmares, when you consider the interpenetration of the Jewish and Ukrainian experience in the geographic territory of Ukraine over the past ten centuries, then the nightmare, for both, becomes further compounded. In our previous paper, we try to grapple with these major historical questions. We conclude that Jews, in terms of their own perceptions of themselves and their relations to Ukrainians, betray a certain — let us call it — 'philosophy of history.' That is to say, an orientation to their own past and to that past as it relates to Ukrainians which provokes a complex set of feelings of animosity, confusion, bitterness and even enmity. Likewise, we discovered that Ukrainians in their 'philosophy of history', that is, their orientations to their own past and that past in relation to Jews, also betray a complex set of feelings, of betrayal,

---

[3] A conference devoted to the fuller explanation of Jewish-Ukrainian Relations is scheduled for October 18-20, 1983 to be held at McMaster University, Hamilton, Ontario. Scholars from Canada, the United States and Israel will spend three days exploring the topic.

exploitation, and treachery.⁴ It is clear to us that we cannot undo history, or that it is extremely difficult to escape from our own 'philosophies of history.' But, as Stephen Daedalus claims, we can at least try to awake from the nightmare of history. In considereing Jewish-Ukrainian relations constructively, we must at least try to find that common ground, both in the past and in the present, upon which we can begin to construct some common projects for understanding, action and interaction. This paper is an attempt to do this.

How do we begin? First, it is important that we understand the complex social, political and economic structures of both the Jewish and Ukrainian communities which lived contiguously for over ten centuries and which mitigated against constructive and salutary relations between these two communities. Let us identify briefly some of these factors. For many centuries, Jews lived in Ukraine as an autonomous community. That autonomy was granted to Jewish communities by foreign rulers in Ukraine, namely the Polish Kingdom. While this communal autonomy ensured the viability of the Jewish communities in Ukraine, it also acted as a major deterrent to any possible relations between Jews and Ukrainians. Second, for almost eight centuries, during the era of the domination of religious orders and feudal structures, the separateness of Jews and Ukrainians was re-inforced by religious differentiation. It is only during the

---

⁴ It would be very interesting and rewarding to try to develop the argument about the thematic unity of the manner in which people view their own history and the history of other people. That is to say, to explore, the subjective interpretation of history of specific peoples or cultural groups.

A very valuable example of this can be found in *History and Jewish Historians: Essays and Addresses by Solo W. Baron*, compiled by Arthur Hertzberg and Leon A. Feldman, Philadelphia, Jewish Publication Society, 1964. Indeed, Baron's work is probably the most important source in how Jews view their own history and how they view the Gentile world. Baron's own thesis is that the Jewish image of their own history as a sealed community is not true even for the most closed ghettos. Jewish history must be understood as part of human history, in general. Baron argues that the Jew should not be viewed as a "pariah" always in a position of otherness. Moreover, the field of Jewish history should be very extensive. Baron's seminal work is found in his many-volumed *A Social and Religious History of the Jews*.

An interesting new example of this effort at defining the thematic unity of Jewish history can be found in Ellis Rivkin, *The Shaping of Jewish History: A Radical New Interpretation*, N.Y., Charles Scribner's Sons, 1971.

Another valuable source is the collection of essays found in H.H. Ben-Sasson and S. Ettinger, eds., *Jewish-Society Through the Ages*, N.Y., Schocken Books, 1971.

latter part of the 18th century and throughout the 19th century, that the tidal waves of secularization broke down these feudal structures and religious differentiations. Third, the separateness of the Jewish and Ukrainian communities was further re-inforced by a complex system of differentiated economic activity. Ukrainians were cast in the role of a 'peasant people' for many, many centuries. They laboured and toiled as a peasant society and found themselves constantly under the yoke of foreign rulers. The Jewish community in Ukraine, however, for a variety of historical circumstances, never found itself cast in the role of a 'peasant people.' Their economic activities and structures meant that they were traders, tax collectors, a more urbanized and commercialized community. The curcial point to remember is that Jews and Ukrainians lived in two, totally differentiated economic structures which, once again, re-inforced their separateness.

Finally, it is important to remember that the Jewish community and the Ukrainians, for many, many centuries stood in different relations to the existing ruling political structures. The Jewish community until the 19th century lived in a kind of protectorate condition to the ruling political structures which were always foreign to the Ukrainian peasant population in Ukraine. As a protectorate population Jews lived under the aegis of a ruling political structure and acted in concert with that ruling structure. The Ukrainian population, however, found itself in a condition of oppression and, at certain points in time, rose up in open opposition and revolt to that ruling structure. During these periods of revolt, the Jewish community found itself caught in violent conflict and cataclysmic upheavals between the rebellious Ukrainian peasantry. These factors compounded the distinctiveness and the separateness of the Jewish and the Ukrainian communities. They provide us with the fundamental realities which fixed the relations — or the non-relations — between Jewish and Ukrainian communities for many centuries. Moreover, these factors help us to understand the circumstances from which each community was able to define a certain set of perceptions of each other.[5]

---

[5] See for example, Jacob Katz, *Out of the Ghetto: The Social Background of Jewish Emancipation, 1770-1870*, Cambridge Mass., Harvard University Press, 1973, Jacob Katz, *Exclusiveness and Tolerance: Studies in Jewish-Gentile Relations in Medieval and Modern Times*, London, Oxford University Press, 1961, Salo W. Baron, *The Jewish Community: Its History and Structure*, Philadelphia, Jewish Publications Society, 1942.

INTO THE TWENTIETH CENTURY: JEWS

We have seen how Jewish-Ukrainian relations were, in a sense, frozen into and by history, with each group viewing each other in terms of a specific and well-defined 'philosophy of history.' Moreover, the social and economic orders reinforced each groups' perception of each other. Each group existed in what may be termed a 'traditional' socio-economic structure which confirmed their perceptions of each other and which reinforced their separateness.

The advent of the 19th century brought massive changes to the entire European continent and also to East Europe. Indeed, modernity, as it is called, rolled through the entire continent from west to east and, in its wake, shattered traditional structures, religious institutions, accepted patterns of economic activity and previously sacred political beliefs. The tumult and changes brought on by the 19th century transformed both the Jewish community living in the Ukrainian region, as well as the Ukrainian community. Why is this important? These transformations provided the opportunity for both communities to free themselves from their historical legacies, to carve new opportunities an chapters in their historical relationships. Indeed, it is during the late 19th and early 20th centuries that we begin to see a fascinating coincidence of political objectives between the Ukrainian community and the Jewish community. The tides of reform, socialism, secularization, nationalism, trade unionism, and most importantly, national autonomy all begin to appear as part and parcel of the socio-political development of both Jewish and Ukrainian communities.[6]

If this historical period is significant as an opportunity for collaboration, it is vital that we examine, in some detail, what was the measure and character of the co-operation between Jews and Ukrainians in this period? Was it successful? Why and how did it fail? What are some of the lessons which we may draw out of this particular period?

---

[6] See for example Jacob S. Raisin, *The Haskalah Movement in Russia*, Philadelphia, Jewish Publication Society 1913, Henry J. Tobias, *The Jewish Bund in Russia from Its Origins to 1905*, Stanford, Stanford University Press, 1972, Robert J. Bryan, *The Jewish Intelligentsia and Russian Marxism*, London, Macmillan, 1978, especially chapter 2, pp. 9-35, Ezra Mendelsohn, *Class Struggle in the Pale: The Formative Years of the Jewish Worker's Movement in Tsarist Russia*, Cambridge, Cambridge University Press, 1970 and the essays entitled "The Hassidic Movement — Reality and Ideals," by S. Ettinger, "The Jewish National Movement: A Sociological Analysis", by Jacob Katz and "The Jewish Labour Movement and European Socialism", by Moshe Mishkinsky, pp. 251-197 in H.H. Ben-Sasson and S. Ettinger, eds., *Jewish Society Through the Ages*, *op. cit.*

In our previous paper, we explored the fundamental structure of the Jewish community in the Ukrainian region prior to the 19th century. Its major characteristics were that it was a fundamentally inward-looking, self-contained community, which regulated itself and was immune from the pressures of the community around it. This community had a juridical basis, defined as a separate community in the hierarchy of the different estates, orders and kingdoms of the time; this community had a segregated and distinctive economic structure, assigned to it by the nature of the kingdoms of the time; the community possessed its own language, educational system, court system, and laws. The pattern of stability, followed by massacre and then a re-birth of messianism was the fundamental historical perspective within which Jews survived.

However, during the period from 1780 to 1880, "Jewish communities underwent a transformation that changed their legal status, their occupational distribution, their cultural habits, as well as their religious outlook and behaviour. The process has been referred to by contemporaries of that time, and by historians in retrospect as well, by different terms: naturalization, reform, civic betterment, amalgamation, assimilation, emancipation.... In all these respects, Jews moved from their former distinct Jewish pattern toward the standard common in their non-Jewish surroundings...the result of the political, social and cultural changes was not the disintegration of the Jewish community but its thorough transformation...."[7] While this process of transformation occurred in Western Europe, it also permeates the Russian Empire, somewhat later. The precess of enlightenment took place in the Russian Empire only in the 1840s and 1860s. In effect, we are dealing with the same sort of transformations, except that it roots itself in the Russian Empire somewhat later than in Western Europe.

The forces leading up to the transformation of Jewish community life arose, peculiarly, in their original form, from within the Jewish community. "Rabbinic Judaism, which has for centuries exercised a powerful hegemony over East European Jewry, was in the eighteenth century assaulted from east and west. *Hasidism*, a revolutionary movement of religious renewal, arose in the Ukrainian provinces of Podolia and Volhynia. *Haskalah*, or enlightenment, began in Berlin, the Prussian capital and the centre of emergent German nationalism."[8]

---

[7] Jacob Katz, *Out of the Ghetto: The Social Background of Jewish Emancipation, op. cit.*, pp. 1-2.

[8] Lucy S. Davidowicz, *The Golden Tradition: Jewish Life and Thought in Eastern Europe*, N.Y., Holt, Rinehart & Winston, 1967, p. 14.

Although both these movements are dramatically different, there are some significant similarities between them which established the fertile ground for the latter intellectual and ideological movements which were to sweep through the Jewish community in East and Central Europe. First, both movements placed emphasis upon the individual, his intrinsic dignity, the importance of his relations to his fellow man and his God. Furthermore, both movements contested and weakened the basis of traditional communal leadership. Both preached the doctrine of equality, meaning different things, of course. *Hasidism* preached equality of all in spiritual liberation, that both rich and poor alike could achieve liberation. The *Maskilim* of the *Haskalah*, preached the doctrine of civic equality, that Jews were willing and able to take their place with others in the responsibilities and duties of citizenship. Both these movements had a profound impact upon the traditional Jewish society of East-Central Europe.

By the second and third decade of the 19th century, there were significant signs of transformation and change in Jewish society. First, the structure of the Jewish family, which had been the fulcrum for stability and continuity, came under pressure from both the *Haskalah* and *Hasidik* movements. Disputes between modernists and traditionalists broke the solidarity which had governed Jewish family life for centuries. Second, the traditional economic structure of Jewish society was changing. As urbanization and industrialization set in, Jews began to enter new professions and businesses. They found their way into the textile industry, sugar production, railroad building, etc. They began operating liquor licenses which had become a government monopoly and Jews secured the licenses. The *Haskalah* movement was thus seen as a practical, reform minded movement which stressed the utilitarian values of work, adaptation and worldly skills in business and commerce.[9] The *Maskilim* wanted to modernize both the school system and the synagogue in order to enable the Jewish community to cope better with the emerging dimensions of modernity.

In 1825, Tsar Nicholas I came to power following the Decembrist uprising. This period coincides with a vast and punative set of actions against the Jews. Nicholas decreed the expulsion of the Jews from their villages; exorbitant taxes were imposed on them; the self-governing *kehillot* were abolished; all but two of the Hewbrew presses were closed down and censorship was imposed; the conscription law of 1827 demanded that Jews serve for 25 years; and in 1844, crown schools for Jews were established in order to control their education.

---

[9] See *Economic History of the Jews*, edited by Nochum Gross, Jerusalem, Keter Publishing Ltd., 1975 for a survey of the development of the economic activity of Jews.

The revolutions that swept Europe in 1848, the death of Nicholas I in 1855 and his succession by Alexander II all signaled a time of major political and economic change which deeply affected Jewish communities. Jews benefitted directly from the reforms in each country and they entered and prospered in the new economic pursuits; they embraced the new patriotism of their lands; they participated actively and feverishly in the culture of these lands. From 1861, with the freeing of the Russian serfs and the liberalization of policies towards the Jews, until 1881, the Jewish communities experienced major changes. Jews benefitted from the liberalization of entry into universities; they entered and prospered in new professions. They had the right to hold office. Jews, as part of the emerging middle class prosperity of this period, began to endorse the ideals of rationalism, science, progress and reform. They began also to participate in the Populist movement, that specifically Russian verion of agrarian socialism which placed the peasant commune at the centre of a reconstructed social order. The secularized currents of socialism and reform swept through some Jewish circles. Aaron Lieberman, (1842-1880) for example, was a Jewish Populist who preached socialism in Hebrew to the Jews. Other significant Jewish Populists were Joseph Aptekman and Solomon Wittenberg.[10]

The assassination of Alexander II in 1881, the ascent to power of Alexander III, the end of reform and the outbreak of pogroms that continued into 1882, destroyed all visions of hope for Jewish emancipation within an enlightened Russian Empire. Lucy Davidowicz argues that "Like a prism, 1881 refracted the Jewish experiences of the past and bent them in another direction. Not since 1648 had the consciousness of being Jewish in an alien and hostile world been so vivid. First the paralyzing shock, then the visceral reaction: flight."[11] From that point onwards, Jews sought ways of escaping. The result was massive emigration over the next three decades to the U.S. As well, the *Bilu Society* was organized in 1882 to colonize Palestine. Although unsuccessful, Davidowicz claims that "*Bilu* signalled the beginning of a new Jewish nationalism."[12]

---

[10] See Louis Greenberg, *The Jewish in Russia: The Struggle for Emancipation*, New Haven, Yale University Press 1944, especially pp. 155-157, and 150-151 for a discussion of Lieberman, Aptekman and Wittenberg. On Lieberman see also *Nationalism and the Class Struggle: A Marxism Approach to the Jewish Problem*, selected writings by Ben Borochor, Westport, Conn.; Greenwood Press, 1972.

[11] Lucy S. Davidowicz, *The Golden Tradition: Jewish Life and Thought in Eastern Europe*, op. cit., p. 47.

[12] *Ibid*, p. 49.

The period following the pogroms of 1881 also coincided with the rebirth of anti-semitism in Europe. Jews throughout Europe faced an uncertain future. In the midst of the swirling changes of industrialization, the cycle of reform and repression, the tides of nationalism, the hopes of socialism and the realities of militarism and repression, Jewish communities became the laboratories of debate, experimentation, action, emigration and re-action. It is during the last two decades of the 19th century and the first decades of the 20th century that one finds the greatest upheavals, intellectual confrontations and passionate disputation among Jews about theories to preserve national Jewish existence in the modern world. The leaders and innovators in these debates were those who had lived through the *Haskalah* movement. It appeared that Jews could face modernity in three ways. First, they could escape, mainly to America, which they did in massive numbers. Second, they could renounce modernity and try to return to traditional piety, with its acceptance of the cycles of hardships, massacres, pogroms, deprivations and seek to live out one's life in this world of Gentile barbarism, obedient to the laws of God and the traditions of one's community. The third possibility was the signal achievement of the Jewish confrontation with the forces of modernity. This was the rise of the major movements which sought a resolution to the problems of Jewish life in the latter half of the 19th century, namely Bundism, Socialism, Zionism, Yiddishism, Hebraism and national autonomism.

The Jewish community of the latter part of the 19th century in East Europe was far from monolithic. It was a community in turmoil and transformation. Jews sought solutions to their dilemmas in all ways outlined above. The first two alternatives, accepted by many Jews, resolved Jewish relations with their neighbours in one direction — namely differentiation and a severence of relationship. It is in the third set of alternatives that we find a fascinating cauldron of possibilities, alliances, proposals for reconciliation and possible co-operation between Jews and their neighbours. It is probably true to say that at no time in history have Jews been such innovators in social theory and political proposals as during this period.[13]

---

[13] The best source, both substantive and bibliographic on this subject is found in Jonathan Frankel's excellent study, *Prophecy and Politics: Socialism, Nationalism and The Russian Jews, 1862-1917*, Cambridge, Cambridge University Press, 1981.

History has a way of resolving intellectual options in unequivocal manners. From the end of the First World War, until the end of the Second World War, most of the options considered by Jews, such as national autonomy, Bundism, Yiddishism, etc. were dramatically destroyed. From the ashes of the Second World War emerged the only viable and triumphant Jewish alternative, namely Zionism. However, it is during this prior period of intellectual options, that we must examine the possibilities of Jewish-Ukrainian co-operation.

INTO THE TWENTIETH CENTURY: UKRAINIANS

In many ways, the transformations of the Jewish communities from the late 18th century on, were paralleled in Ukrainian society, in general. The story of Ukraine since the end of the eighteenth century is the story of the challenges which the forces of modernity posed to traditional Ukrainian ways, of the impact they had on the Ukrainian people, and of the manner in which Ukrainian responded to them.

The beginnings of the modern period in Ukrainian history coincided with profound changes in power relations in eastern and central Europe which critically affected Ukraine's subsequent development.

The partitions of Poland meant that the Right Bank Ukraine was annexed by Russia, while Galicia, Bukovina and Transcarpathia became parts of Austria-Hungary. These territorial arrangements remained virtually unchanged for more than a hundred years or until the First World War. Within this splintered setting, the Ukrainian national revival took place. Various scholars divide the history of the Ukrainian national revival into a number of stages. I.L. Rudnytsky, for example separates it into three periods: a) pre-1840s (The Period of Nobility); b) 1840-1880 (The Populist Period); c) 1890-1917 (The Modern Period).[14] O. Pritsak and J.S. Reshetar, Jr., suggest: 1) The Novhorod-Siversk

---

[14] I.L. Rudnytsky, *Mizh istorieiu i politykoiu*, Suchasnist 1973, pp. 76-79; For a more exhaustive treatment of these questions see: M. Hrushevskyi, *Kul'turno-natsional'yni rukh na Ukraini V XVI-XVII* v. Kiev, 1912 j V. Diadychenko, *Narysy suspil'no-politychnoho ustroiu Livoberezhnoi Ukrainy* kintsia XVII-pochatku XVIII st., Kiev, 1959; A. Pypin, *Obshchestvennoe dvizhenie v Rossii pri Aleksandre I*, Petrognod, 1918; V. Okhrymovych, *Rozvytok Ukrains'koi natsional'no-politychnoi dumky*, Lviv, 1922; O. Hermaize, *Narysy a istorii revoliutsiinoho rukhu na Ukraini*, Kiev, 1926; M. Iavors'kyi, *Narysy z istorii Revlouitsiinoi Borot'by na Ukraini*, 2 vols. Kharkiv, 1927-28; F. Savchenko, *Zaborona Ukrainstva 1876r*, Kiev 1930; D. Doroshenko, *Z istorii Ukrains'koi politychnoi dumky za chasiv svitovoi viiny*, Prague, 1936; K. Levyts'kyi, *Isoriia politychnoi dumky halyts'kykh ukraintsiv, 1848-1918*, 2 vols; Lviv, 1926-27; H. Herbil's'kyi, *Peredova supil'na dumka v Halyhyni: 30-i seredyna 40-kh rokiv XIX stolittia*, Lviv, 1959;

stage and the *Istoriia Rusov*; 2) The Kharkov stage and the beginning of political movement; 3) The Kiev Stage and the beginning of political movement; 4) The Geneva Stage and M. Drahomanov; and 5) The Galician Stage and the formation of the first Ukrainian political party.[15] R. Szporluk suggests three overlapping phases: a) academic, b) cultural, and c) political.[16]

The academic phase (which coincides partially with Rudnytsky's pre-populist period) began in the 1780s at the time when many educated Ukrainians believed that a distinct Ukrainian nationality ceased to exist and together with it, the language and the folk culture of Ukraine. In order to preserve the memory of Ukraine, they began to collect historical documents, folk songs, legends and artifacts of various kinds and to write scholarly studies in history, linguistics, literature and ethnography. These efforts made possible the later recognition of Ukraine as a distinct nation in the sense in which nationality was becoming understood in Europe in the late 18th and early 19th century i.e. "as a community of people based on a common language, culture and history." From this it was easy "to draw the conclusions that every nation so defined was entitled to be recognized as such, and in the final analysis, could even claim political independence."[17]

The second phase of national development, the cultural, which coincides more or less with Rudnytsky's Populist period, is marked by adoption of the vernacular as the literary language. The first writer who had the courage to write in the vernacular rather than in the old Church Slavonic was Ivan Kotliarevskyi (1769-1838). "This epoch-making step, symbolized by the publication of his *Eneida* in 1798, initiated a transformation which for Ukraine was as significant as the elimination in the West of Latin as the literary medium."[18] Taras Shevchenko (1814-1861), the greatest Ukrainian poet of all times, developed and enriched the new Ukrainian literary language even further. But his greatest achievement was that "he created in fully poetic form not only the vision of an independent Ukraine (separate fro Catholic Poland and Orthodox Russia) but also the idea of an armed struggle for its attainment."[19]

---

[15] O. Pritsak and J.S. Reshetar Jr., "The Ukraine and the Dialectics of Nation Building", in D.W. Treadgold, ed., *The Development of the USSR: An Exchange of Views*, Seattle, 1964, pp. 236-267.

[16] R. Szporluk, *Ukraine: A Brief History*, Detroit, 1979, p. 41.

[17] *Ibid*, p. 42. Some of the important figures of that period are O. Rignel'man, J. Poletyka, D. Bantysh-Kamenskyi, M. Markevych, O. Pavlovskyi, M. Maksymovych and the anonymous author of *Istoriia Rusov*.

[18] John S. Reshetar Jr., *The Ukrainian Revolution, 1917-1920: A Study in Nationalism*, Princeton, 1952, p. 5.

[19] O. Pritsak and J.S. Reshetar Jr., "The Ukraine and the Dialectic of Nation Building", *op. cit.*, p. 264.

Shevchenko joined with other like-minded Ukrainians, such as N. Kostomarov and P. Kulish, in founding the Society of Saints Cyril and Methodius in Kiev, in 1846. This society sought the establishment of a confederation of self-governing Slavic republics composed of legally equal units. It also advocated the abolition of serfdom, corporal punishment, illiteracy, and the guarantee of freedom of conscience, press and speech. It also called for an end to religious animosities. Discovered by the Tsarist police, the Society members were arrested (Shevchenko was sentenced to 10 years of exile in Kirgizia) and the activities of the Society were terminated in 1847. Thus, the first modern Ukrainian political movement came to an early end and was not to be succeeded by any similar endeavor for several decades.

The Imperial Russian Government used its full force to restrict the use of Ukrainian. In 1863 and again in 1876 the authorities prohibited the use of the Ukrainian language in books and periodical publishing, on stage and in schools. "These prohibitions served a clear purpose: to prevent the transformation of Ukrainian folk culture, associated with the world of the village, into a modern culture which would appeal to educated, urban people. The government wanted to prevent the emergence of such class functioning professionally in the Ukrainian language, which might form the basis of a nationalist movement."[20]

The second figure who contributed greatly to the development of the Ukrainian national awakening was M.P. Drahomanov (1841-1895). He insisted that the Ukrainian movement could not remain apolitical and purely cultural, that all political movements in Ukraine had to have Ukrainian national character, and that the Ukraine had to have Ukrainian national character, and that the Ukrainian nation had a right to complete equality. Drahomanov also expressed the view that emigration was not a viable solution to the question of the future of Jewish national life. In his exchanges with Ben Ami, he argues that "Russian is not Switzerland or even Germany — in the western part of Russia there are at least 3,000,000 Jews. That is an entire nation".[21] Jewish intellectuals must remain rooted in their own community and remain true to their own language Yiddish, and culture. To Drahomanov, all attempts at internationalism would lead simply to Russification for both Jews and Ukrainians alike.

---

[20] R. Szporluk, *op. cit.*, p. 46.

[21] Ivan L. Rudnytsky, ed., *Mykhailo Drahomanov: A Symposium and Selected Writings*, Vol. II, No. 1 (1952) of *The Annals of the Ukrainian Academy of Arts and Sciences in the U.S.*, and for some valuable discussions of Drahomanov, see Jonathan Frankel, *Prophecy and Politics: Socialism, Nationalism and The Russian Jews*, 1862-1917, Cambridge, Cambridge University Press, 1981, pp. 101-113. See also, John-Paul Himka's excellent biography of Drahomanov in Joseph L. Wieczynski, ed. *The Modern Encylopedia of Russian and Soviet History*, Academic International Press, 1979, Vol. 10, pp. 7-9.

The third phase, the political stage 1890-1917, in Ukrainian history is very important in the further development of the Ukrainian national consciousness and political thought.

Two factors had tremendous influence on Ukrainian developments in this period. First, there was the increasing weakening of the Tsarist absolutism and the deterioration of the Russian state machinery. Second, there was rapid economic developments in Ukraine, including industrialization and the rise in the living standards of the people, generally. Of course, at the same time, there occurred such processes as the *proletarianization* of the poor peasantry. These factors sharpened the social contradictions in the country. This period was reflected not only in the growth of political parties but also in a great deal of party differentiation.[22]

---

[22] For a more detailed approach see: M. Slabchenko, *Khoziastvo Getmanshchiny V XVII-XVIII st.*, I-IV, Odessa, 1922-25; A. Obloblin (Ohloblyn), *Ocherki istorii ukrainskoi fabriki: Predkapitalisticheskaia fabrika*, Kiev, 1925; O. Ohloblyn, *Narysy a istorii kapitalizmu na Ukraini*, Kharkiv-Kiev, 1931; N. Polons'ka-Vasylenko, "The Settlement of the Southern Ukraine, 1950-75," *Annals of Ukrainian Academy of Arts and Sciences*, Vol. IV-V, New York, 1955; O. Nesterenko, *Rozvyrok promyslovosti na Ukraini*, Kiev, 1959; B. Veselovskyi, *Istoriia zemstva za yo let*, I-IV, St. Petersburg, 1909-11; P. Gronsky, *The Zemstvo System and Local Government in Russia*, New York, 1923; M. Slabchenko, *Materialy do ekonomichno-sotsial'noi istorii Ukrainy XIX st.*, 2 vols., Odessa, 1925-27; M. Slabchenko, *Borot'ba za systemy zemlevolodinnia i formy hospodarstva v Ukraini XIX-XX stolittia*, Odessa, 1927; V. Dubrovs'kyi, *Selians'ki rukhy na Ukraini pislia 1861 r*, Kharkiv, 1928; I. Hurzhii, *Rozklad feodal'no.-kriposnyts'koi systemy v sil's'komu hospodarstvi Ukrainy pershoi polovyny XIX st.*, Kiev, 1954; *Formirovanie raobchego klassa na Ukraine i ego revoliutsionnaia bor'ba v kontse XIX i v nachale XX v.*, Kiev, 1956; K. Kononenko, *Ukraine and Russia: A History of the Economic Relations Between Ukraine and Russia, 1654-1917*, Milwaukee, 1958; N. Leshchenko, *Krestianskoe dvizhenie na Ukraine v sviazi s provedeniem reformy 1861 goda*, Kiev, 1959; V. Teplyts'kyi, *Reforma 1861 roku i ahrarni vidnosyny na Ukraini*, Kiev, 1959; *Z istorii suspil'no-ekonomichnoho rozvytky ta klasovoi borot'by na Ukraini (XVI-pochatok XX st.) Naukovi Zapysky Instytutu Istorii AN USSR, XIII*, Kiev, 1960; I. Hurzhii, *Rozvytok tovarnoho vyrobnytstva i torhivli na Ukraini*, Kiev, 1962; A. Krevets'kyi, *Agrarni boikoty i straiky u Skhidnii Halychyni v 1848-49 rr.*, Lviv, 1906; I. Franko, *Panshchyna i ii skasuvannia v 1848 r. v Halychyni*, Lviv, 1913; Ri Kann, *The Multinational Empire: Nationalism and National Reform in the Hobsbury Monarchy 1848-1918*, 2 vols. New York, 1950; M. Herasymenko, *Ahrarni vidnosyny v Halychyni v period kryzy panshchynnoho hospodarstva*, Kiev, 1959; D. Kvitkovs'kyi,et al eds., *Bukovyna ii mynule i suchasne*, Paris, 1958; ;O. Mytsiuk, *Narysy z sotsial'no-hospodars'koi istorii Pidkarpats'koi Rusy*, Prague, 1938; S. Ostapenko, *Kapitalizm na Ukraini*, Kharkiv, 1925; V. Osechyns'yi, *Halychyna pid*

The first important movement was the secret Taras Brotherhood (*Bratstvo Tarasivtsiv*) which was founded in 1891 on Shevchenko's grave at Kaniv by men who did not wish to enter Russian political parties. Their programme called for "the liberation of all peoples in Russia from despotism and centralism and the granting of autonomy, promotion of the public welfare, and establishment of a social system having neither exploiters nor exploited."[23]

In 1899, in Kharkov, was founded the Revolutionary Ukrainian Party which later on shifted to Marxism and became the Ukrainian Social-Democratic Workers Party. After 1905 we see the beginnings of other parties: the liberal (Radical-Democrats); the agrarian the socialist (Socialist-Revolutionaries) and the nationalist (Ukrainian Peoples Party). These parties did not have time to develop fully and by 1907 many of them were driven underground.[24] What is important to note is that the socio-economic developments in Ukrainian society resulted in political differentiation, as well.

The Revolution of 1905 is significant because it created the conditions whereby the intelligentsia, previously separated from the population, could now work openly with them. The smaller towns and villages of Ukraine were covered by a network of *Prosvitas* (Enlightenment societies), and cooperatives began to serve as the vital points for political movement. The growth of a village intelligentsia, such as cooperative organizers, teachers, local health officials, agronomists, etc., themselves of peasant origin, exerted tremendous influence on the village population who trusted them implicitly.

---

hnitom Avstro-Uhorshchyny v epokhu imperialismu, Lviv, 1954; I. Kompaniet's, *Stanovyshche i borot'ba trudiashchykh mas Halychyny, Bukovyny i Zakarpattia na pochatku XX st. (1900-1919)*, Kiev, 1961; I. Shul'ha, *Sotsial'no'Ekonomichni vidnosyny i klasova borot'ba na Zakarpatti v kintsi XVIII-pershii polovyni XIX st.*, Lviv, 1965 A. Porits'kyi, *Pobut sil's'ko-hospodars'kykh robitnykiv Urkrainy v period kapitalizmu*, Kiev, 1964; V.A. Diadychenko, ed., *Istoriia selianstva Ukrainskoi SSR*, 2 vols., Kiev, 1967; F.E. Los', *Istoriia robitnychoho klasu Ukrains'koi SSR*, 2 vols, Kiev, 1967.

For an English language material on general socio-economic and political conditions in Ukrainian territories see: *Ukraine a Concise Encyclopaediia*, Toronto, 1971, Vol II, pp; 695-699; 750-759; 840-849; 895-900; 952-958; 978-984; 989-990; 1011-1018; 1031-1034. On scholarship and education and schools see: *ibid*, pp. 238-252; 308-343.

[23] J.S. Reshetar, Jr., *The Ukrainian Revolution, op. cit.*, p. 12.

[24] For a detailed study of these developments see Jury Borys,, *The Sovietization of Ukraine: 1917-1923*, Revised Edition, Edmonton, 1980, chapter III, pp. 74-97, 98-120.

The national idea began to permeate other social classes, as well, although not as rapidly. Long before 1914, there are indications that the workers began to show clear interests in th national question.[25] The same was true among the bourgeoisie and the town's people, although here regional consciousness was, perhaps, more important. The Revolution of 1917 speeded up the dynamics of this process but, at the same time, it did not allow sufficient time for its growth and maturity. However, the notion of national autonomy was widely known abd fully acceptable by a wide range of people, movements and parties. While national autonomy was the predominant view in the minds of Ukrainians in the Russian Empire, in Ukrainian lands in the Austro-Hungarian Empire this view was extended to embrace the idea of independence. For many decades Ukrainian life in Austro-Hungary was freer, more open and the permutations of political ideals more advanced. By 1917 Ukrainians in Galicia has already advanced the option of independence for all Ukrainians.

POINTS OF INTERSECTION: NATIONAL AUTONOMY

We have seen how the forces of modernization deeply affected the traditional structures of both the Ukrainian and Jewish communities. On the political level, both communities developed a variety of political movements, parties and leaders which espoused different solutions to the political dilemmas facing each community. The processes of political fragmentation proceeded unabaited through the early part of the 20th century.

While it is possible to analyze these movements, parties, etc., along a variety of dimensions, what is of concern to us is to identify the points at which there is an intersection, coincidence, or similarity in proposals which emanated from the Jewish and Ukrainian communities simultaneously. This crucial point of intersection is the notion of national autonomy.

Why is this idea crucial and what does it indicate to us about the possibilities of Jewish-Ukrainian relations? In viewing the long history of Jewish-Ukrainian relations, there are very few, if any, points at which Jewish and Ukrainian perspectives and interests coincide. Indeed, as we have argued previously, the fundamental difficulty in Jewish-Ukrainian relations has to do with the failure of the coincidence of interests and perspectives. In the political cauldron of the first

---

[25] "Nakaz deputatu IV Gossudarstvennoi Cumy G.I. Petrovskomu ot Ekaterinoslavskikh rabochikh o zashchite prav ukrainskogo naseleniia", in Rabochee Dvizhenie na Ukraine v Gody Novogo Revoliutsiogo Podema, 1910-1914, Kiev, 1959, p. 363.

part of this century in Ukrainian regions within the Russian and Austro-Hungarian Empires, we witness, for the first time, the coincidence of interests and perspectives on fundamental political problems from both the Jewish and Ukrainian communities. As we have shown previously, the cycle of emancipation and then repression, the tides of secularization and industrial development, the growing pre-occupations with the question of national fate and the solution to the national question — all these problems and forces affected both Ukrainians and Jews alike. And, moreover, the resultant fragmentation of political forces occurred in both communities. Within this fragmentation, the idea of national autonomy appears as the singular idea which binds Ukrainian and Jewish interests together. Obviously, the idea, itself, is therefore worth studying because it identifies the common ground on which Jewish-Ukrainian relations co-existed for some time.

There is, however, a second and more dramatic reason as to why the notion of national autonomy is critical in Jewish-Ukrainian relations. From the years 1917-1920, national autonomy was more than an idea in the Ukrainian region. During this period, national autonomy emerged as the political practice and the basis for the fashioning of critical institutions. It evolved as a critical prototype of the kind of political formations possible for ethnically divided societies. This crucial experiment in what we, as Canadians, might call institutionalized and politicized multiculturalism within a federal state did not last very long, unfortunately. But, clearly, it is a concept which found its way into the heart and centre of the experiment of Ukrainian independence, short-lived as it was.

The idea of national autonomy emerged in the latter part of the 19th century as the logical political proposal in situations where the tides of nationalism met the realities of disintegrating empires. In East and Central Europe, these two forces coincided and the notion of national autonomy, therefore, took hold in many regions. The fundamental tenet of national autonomy was that certain groups constituted a nationality and that nationality expressed itself through a specific language and a specific set of cultural expressions. Moreover, each national grouping had a right to define a set of political relations within which their linguistic and cultural expressions would be ensured and could flourish. The tortuous questions for most national groups was to define the nature of those political relations. Some groups argued that only within the context of political independence could the national groups ensure their long term viability in linguistic and cultural terms. Others argued that this viability could be assured within a kind of quasi-federal system, so that a variety of national groups could share equally the same set of political institutions and yet, they could preserve their linguistic and cultural qualities. This latter idea emerges as the notion of national autonomy. Obviously, there is a logical extension from the notion of national autonomy to the notion of political independence. Indeed there are many movements individuals and groups, both within the Jewish and Ukrainian communities which moved from one concept to the next. If one endorsed the notion of political independence. Then the collaborative possibilities between Jews and Ukrainians was minimized. Each national group must undertake its own struggle for political independence. If, however, one adopted and endorsed the option of national autonomy within a quasi-federal political structure, then, obviously, there was significant room for close collaboration between Jews and Ukrainians. The period 1917-1920 was the critical period where these two options were debated, acted upon and put into political practice in Ukraine. How did this come about?

Between 1905-1910, national autonomy became the fundamental principle of all modern Jewish movements. Jonathan Frankel, for example, argues that "Although Dubnov and Zhitlovsky were the first to advocate the idea of autonomism (or extraterritorial self-government), the Bund alone took it up at an early stage (in 1901) and thus leant it great weight. It was adopted in the years 1905-06 by nearly all the Jewish parties in Russia and in 1918 (as 'national rights') by the leaders of American Jewry. Via this route it found its way in 1919-20 into the Paris Peace Treaties, which dealt with the newly independent states of non-Soviet eastern Europe. Jewish autonomism was explicitly rejected by the Bolshevik regime."[26]

The history of Jewish cultural autonomy from the March 1917 period to 1920 is both fascinating and instructive. Solomon I. Goldeman's book *Jewish National Autonomy in Ukraine, 1971-1920* is probably the single best source on the subject. Goldelman argues that "Jewish National Autonomy flashed by on the horizon of Jewish life like a brilliant comet; then disappeared without a trace. And of the intense creative work of the democratic Jewish community during the course of four years of revolution there was nothing left but misty reminiscences of something brilliant, that had drowned in dark fear and torment and that was preserved in the national memory from the pogrom era, which came in paradoxical concurrence with the structure of autonomous national life.

---

[26] Jonathan Frankel, *Prophecy and Politics*, op. cit., p. 171. Frankel's book offers us a good discussion of the principles of national autonomism. See also M. Mintz, "The Internationality Secretariat of The Ukrainian General Secretariat, 1917-1918," in *Harvard Ukrainian Studies*, Vol. 6, No. 1, 1982.

Perhaps, one of the most interesting thinkers who approached the idea of national autonomy was Ben Barochov. His work is now available in English in *Nationalism and the Class Struggle: A Marxism Approach to the Jewish Problem*, selected writings by Ben Barochov, Wesport, Conn., Greenwood Press, 1972.

The Jewish National Autonomy and the Ukrainian Revolution came on the scene of events as Siamese twins. With the fall of an independent Ukrainian state there followed automatically an end also to Jewish National Autonomy."[27] The features of national autonomy granted to the Jews in this period were, indeed, impressive. For example, the Central Ukrainian Council (Rada) recognized the rights of its national minorities, including the Jews and provided for them a Statute of National-Personal Autonomy, which was adopted on January 9, 1918. Soon afterwards, there followed a Ministry of Jewish Affairs, with a staff of over 100 persons. The Jews of Ukraine elected a Jewish National Council to develop and institute their cultural politics.

Throughout east and central Europe, the idea of national autonomy had different forms of development. Most experiments in national autonomy started auspiciously. But throughout eastern Europe, the fate of national autonomy collapsed shortly after 1920 and from its collapse arose rightist reactions and fascist dictatorships.

It is worthwhile noting, however, as Goldelman indicates to us, the "Jewish National Autonomy in Ukraine was not an isolated phenomenon in the Russian revolution. Similar parallel events can be found also within the framework of some of the other national revolutions such as those of Latvia, Lithuania, Estonia, and partly in Bielo-Russia. But when we compare the national achievements of the Jewish minority in those countries with the extent, competence, practical activity, and particularly with the formal constitutional status of Jewish autonomy within the framework of the Ukrainian state, we become cognizant of the exclusive originality of the autonomous status of the Jewish minority in Ukraine, and of the exemplary character of this status. The great extent of national autonomy granted the Jewish minority in Ukraine stands alone in the entire history of the Jewish people in diaspora. It was a distinct and unique example among the attempts to regulate international relations in many multi-national states."[28]

---

[27] Solomon I. Goldelman, *Jewish National Autonomy in Ukraine*, 1917-1920, p. 123.

[28] *Ibid.*, pp. 13-14.

CONCLUSIONS

The period of Ukrainian independence came to an end in 1920 and with it the period of Jewish national autonomy. However, the achievements at this period lasted into the mid 1920s. Both Jewish and Ukrainian communities fell victim to Soviet nationalities policies, Russification and centralized control. By the mid-1920s, Jews and Ukrainians were caught up in a fierce struggle to preserve some small dimensions of cultural and linguistic integrity in the face of massive pressures from the Soviet regime.

The twentieth century is an enormous nightmare for many peoples. In East and Central Europe three people in particular faced the prospect of premeditated and immanent annihiliation — Amenians, Jews and also Ukrainians. From the mid 1920s until 1932, Ukrainian national life was systematically assaulted, their cultural and national institutions continuously destroyed and under the pretext of collectivization, up to six million people perished. In East and Central Europe, by 1945, as a result of Nazism and Stalinist policies, ten centuries of Jewish life in that region came to an end. From the ashes of 1945 emerged the state of Israel in 1948. Ukrainian national life still hangs precariously unresolved to this day. What can we learn from Ukrainian and Jewish history in the 20th century and from that unique period 1917-1920?

First, the apogee, the highest and most accommodating period of Jewish-Ukrainian relations rests in the period 1917-1920. Most significantly, it is in the condition of Ukrainian independence that Jews and Ukrainians were able to fashion a viable and constructive relationship. Or, to put it somewhat differently, for the centuries when Jews and Ukrainians lived contiguously but under foreign domination, Jewish and Ukrainian interests and perspectives could never intersect. When foreign domination was thrown off, then Jews and Ukrainians could construct a salutary relationship. As we have seen, this point of intersection began with the endorsation of the principle of national autonomy. When Ukrainian independence collapsed and the principle of national autonomy was lost, disaster beset both Jews and Ukrainians.

Second, it is worth nothing that during the Second World War, for political reasons, when Russian power was relaxed over the Ukrainian region, the idea of cultural autonomy was once again revived. In 1946, for example, Yuri Smolych, a Ukrainian writer, proposed the revival of Jewish institutions in the context of the revival of the principle of national autonomy. Alas, this idea was again quashed with the attack by Stalin on both Jews and Ukrainians, the first under the guise of "rootless cosmopolitanism" and the second for "bourgeois nationalism."

Third, the same forces have fashioned the history of Jews and Ukrainians in the 19th and 20th centuries. Secularization and the collapse of 19th century empires provoked the forces of nationalism among both Jews and Ukrainians. The struggles for national autonomy and political independence in the face of massive forces of annihiliation are common to both people.

Fourth, while it is true that the state of Israel has resolved the struggles for political independence of Jews to a certain degree, there still remain some 800,000 Jews who live in Ukraine. The question of national autonomy, the right to one's own culture — as the U.N. Charter of Human Rights calls it — is still a political objective which unites both Jews and Ukrainians in the present context of the U.S.S.R. It is at this point where, once again, as in the past, Jews and Ukrainians share a common interest and a common concern.

Fifth, as we have seen, one of the precipitating conditions for strained relations between Jews and Ukrainians is the presence of foreign domination in Ukraine. Only when there was an absence of foreign domination, i.e. during the brief interval of Ukrainian independence, were Jewish-Ukrainian relations established, on what one may term, an equal and salutary basis. One may indeed conclude therefore that only when the conditions of foreign domination are eradicated, for both Jews and Ukrainians, that many of the problems in Jewish-Ukrainian relations may be resolved.

A JEW AND A UKRAINIAN: AUTOBIOGRAPHICAL AFTERTHOUGHTS

Sir Karl Popper, a man who has lived in and through a variety of cultures, was fond of sying that intellectual problems tend to have two origins: first, they originate in the world of the intellect, that abstract world of knowledge which thinkers, scholars and philosophers tend to explore; and, second, they tend to originate in the peculiar constellation of one's own makeup, the nature of one's own autobiography. People tend to become intrigued by problems through the intersection of these two elements.

The essays in this volume involve a dual conjunction. Our concerns and interests in the problems of Jewish-Ukrainian relations arose out of common concerns on an intellectual level with the fate of Jewish-Ukrainian relations. But in the process of exploring this question from an academic point of view, we as individuals, as members of our own communities, as historical creatures and as friends began to explore our own pasts, our own backgrounds.

The essays which have preceded this one in the volume have laid out the groundwork for the problem of Jewish-Ukrainian relations on an intellectual or academic level. This essay is a more personal account of how, why and wherefore we have come to this problem.

HOWARD ASTER: BY WAY OF AUTOBIOGRAPHY

I was born and brought up in Montreal. I come from a working class home. My father was an upholsterer who came to Canada alone, having left behind his mother and two sisters. His father died when he was six years of age. He subsequently worked and managed to bring his mother and two sisters to Canada. Not an unusual story so far!

I was brought up in a working-class, Jewish neighbourhood in Montreal. My father was a typical Jew in the new world. He believed in hard work, devotion to his family and obedience to his God. He also taught his three sons that they had to make a choice in this world. They could follow his path of manual labour, or else they could try to pursue their studies and thus carve out for themselves some other calling in life. His duty was to provide us with the opportunities for education. I attended Talmud Torah public school and then I went on to study at Herzliah High School; always remembering that the choice had to be made between the work of one's hands — as my father, craft — or the work of the mind and the spirit — the intellect. I chose to continue my studies at McGill, Yale and the London School of Economics. Obviously, I chose to pursue the world of the intellect.

My boyhood neighbourhood was a typical Jewish neighbourhood. I attended a Jewish school; on my way there, I passed by a Jewish old people's home; after school, I would go to the Jewish Public Library to study; I played my sports at the Young Men's Hebrew Association; I attended synagogue on holidays in a small neighbourhood 'shule.' My knowledge of institutions and the nature of organized life was always Jewish institutions, Jewish life. I was aware that there were 'other' people around me.

In Montreal, the awareness of those 'other' people meant French-Canadians. They were the 'goyim.' I fought with French-Canadians, at times, on the streets. I knew they had their own community, their own schools, their own churches. I also knew that they would menace me and my Jewish friends from time to time. Street fights were my first encounters with 'goyish' brutality, with anti-semitism, with the experience of 'pogroms.' But my community persisted and thrived. We lived, we went on to better education. And, I confirmed for myself and for my father that the work of the intellect was superior to the work of one's hands.

Upon reflection, the question arises — why is the short sojourn into autobiography important? The answer is simple. My childhood and boyhood experiences were not unique. But they confirmed for me a fundamental understanding of the world around me. And what was that understanding? In simplified terms it was that security resided in my own community. Second, that the 'outside' world was an alien world, a world hostile to Jews. Third, that there was a fundamental distinction to be made between the world of spirit and intellect personified by learning, education, or the highest aspirations of Jewish culture and the world of brutality, anti-semitism, crassness and indiscriminate 'pogroms' which Jewish life, even in Montreal, was subject to. Fourth, that there were very few possibilities for meaningful contact between these two worlds; that the chasm between Jewish life and culture and the 'outside' world was, practically, unbridgeable. To put it in somewhat different terms, the fate of the Jew was to live in a world beset by two solitudes — on the one hand the life of Jewish life and culture and then, the world of 'the others.' There was no reconciliation between these two solitudes, no hope of ever integrating, or unifying these two solitudes.

So, how did I come to Jewish-Ukrainian relations? My professional field as a political scientist is Canadian politics and political theory. I am neither a specialist in Jewish history, nor a specialist in Soviet affairs. I have read and studied aspects of both fields, but I would not claim expertise in either. And yet, over the years of my association with McMaster University, as a member of the Department of Political Science, I have developed an intimate friendship with one colleague, who happens to be Ukrainian. I know his home, his family, his children, his cultural values, his individual and his national aspirations.

My friendship with this individual was a voyage of discovery. It was through him that I learned so much about the culture, the milieu, the character and quality of life from which my father came. He grew up in a town not that distant from where my father spent the first 16 years of his life. Typical of Jews of his generation, my father spoke very sparsely about life in his home town, Koretz. To him, Ukraine was a place that he left behind. It was not a place which he wanted to remember. Indeed, it was a place he wanted to forget. Hence, I knew very little about that 'place.'

To my surprise, I soon came to realize that there were many similarities between the Jewish value systems and Ukrainian value systems. Yes, of course, Jewish food and Ukrainian food are astonishingly similar. But more importantly, I learned from my colleague other things. The reverence of education and the life of the intellect was something which both he and I shared not simply as individuals, but as members of two different communities. I learned that both Jews and Ukrainians live with the past as the present. That is to say, both Jews and Ukrainians revere their histories are minority, oppressed peoples, and both people have tried to establish their own statehood as a solution to the problem of oppression and minority status. I learned that freedom is a value which both peoples embrace. I learned that both communities have a profound commitment to the idea that the 'right to one's own language' is an integral part of the survival of their own communities. I learned about the fate of small nations caught within the vissicitudes of empires and imperial powers. I began to see that history had cast Jews and Ukrainians into many parallel situations and there was a commonality of experience between Jews and Ukrainians which astonished me.

And yet . . . I also remembered from my Jewish cultural upbringing that Ukrainians were a demonic force. That among the demonology of 'goyish' people, Ukrainians were, for Jews, worse than Poles, worse than Germans, even worse than Arabs. I began to wonder, why was this so; how could it be that my own personal experience with my colleague was so diametrically opposite to the received wisdom of my own culture?

How to resolve this conundrum? How to come to grips with this apparent difficulty?

The answer, to a degree, was the effort to write the monograph, entitled *Jewish-Ukrainian Relations: Two Solitudes*.

PETER POTICHNYJ: BY WAY OF AUTOBIOGRAPHY

I was born in Western Ukraine at the time when that region found itself within the borders of the resurrected Polish state. My family, not unlike most Ukrainian families of that time, was caught in the storm of repression and intimidation unleashed by some chauvinist elements in the Polish elite against the Ukrainian population and other ethnic groups and their strivings for cultural and political independence. My father had to spend time, on several occasions, in jail for Ukrainian activities, the last time in the infamous concentration camp Bereza Kartuzska from which he was released at the outbreak of the German-Polish war of September 1939. Brought to a neighbourhood town, Dynow, by the Polish military police, he was in danger of being executed were it not for the bold action of the City Council which was composed almost entirely of Jews, and in particular the Bourgomeister by the name of Liszka. From my mother, I learned that when Mr. Liszka fled from the Germans, he left with our family all of his treasured possessions, the family silver and many albums of pictures. He returned after the Soviets occupied our area to collect his treasures. Our family tried on several occasions to find him but we were unsuccessful.

The fact that on the male side my family, for generations, was considered Polish and Roman Catholic didn't matter at all to the Polish authorities. My father was considered a dangerous nationalist and a traitor because he insisted that his three sons (I am one of the triplets) be baptized in the Ukrainian and not the Polish church. Eventually, he officially transferred his allegiance to the Ukrainian Catholic Church. This was more a political declaration because, I suspect, he was not a very religious person. At least that is the impression I get whenever I raise this question with my very religious mother who now lives in Toronto. She immediately shakes her head and begins to speak in generalities. I am not certain, but I suspect that in the end he also became a member of the OUN, the Ukrainian underground.

1939 was also the year when Hitler and Stalin divided the corpse of Poland between themselves and my part of the country experienced "liberation," this time by the Soviet Union. In this transitional period, when the border between the two imperialists was not yet sealed and the Germans were still moving in, our attic became a safe refuge for many male Jews from the city of Sanok, who were moving east. I was then 9 years old and I remember helping Mother to carry food and milk to them.

A year later, in 1940, my father's teaching career came to an end. He was arrested this time by the Soviet political police and all traces of him disappeared forever. Somewhat later, we were told that he was executed by the Soviet police, who in fear of being overtaken by the advancing Germans, had orders to kill all prisoners. Thousands died in this manner, many of them, like my father, were never actually charged with any specific crimes or sentenced for them. Their bodies were dumped into a salt-well near the city of Dobromyl.

When I was 11, the German-Soviet war began and I remember how happy we all were at first that the Soviet terror was no more. But the Germans did not bring us peace, and freedom but only more terror.

Later on, I was separated from my family, I found myself first in Western Europe, then in the United States and finally in Canada. It was here in Canada that only 10 years ago I saw my family reassembled, with both my brothers and my mother joining me here, hopefully, to live out our remaining years in relative peace and quiet.

So how did I come to Jewish-Ukrainian relations? The Jews were part and parcel of my childhood years. Not as my schoolmates, nor as the children of the neighbourhood with whom one played and fought day in and day out. Yet, the Jews were everywhere. You could tell them by their appearance and the economic roles they played in society.

The first time I identified with a Jew was when I was 9 years old. It so happened that the border between the Germans and the Soviets ran along the river San and the Jews were trying to flee to the Soviet side. Among them was a small boy probably 8 or 9, like myself. He was utterly alone; he was wet and cold, he was frightened and through his tears he was saying in Polish again and again: "I want to go to my aunt in Piatkowa." An old Ukrainian woman came to him, hugged him, gave him something to eat and sent him on his way. I saw myself in this boy's shoes and I never forgot that episode!

The second time which I vividly remember was my experience in Lviv at the end of 1942. I was going to school when along Horodecka Street I encountered a long column of Jews who were being escorted by the Jewish police carrying truncheons and a few German guards armed with rifles. All of a sudden one man in the column bolted and started running along the street. The Jewish policeman caught up with him and hit him with a club. The man staggered but kept running. The German guard then knelt, aimed his rifle and fired. The man fell. I had never before seen a man killed and I was thoroughly shocked. But it wasn't just any man that I saw killed. In my shock and disbelief I imagined that man to be my father. I was 12 years old!

In March 1945 the village of my parents, Pawlokoma, was surrounded by murderous bands and 365 innocent men, women and children were slaughtered simply because they happened to be Ukrainians. My cousin who now lives in Edmonton, lost her father and five brothers in that slaughter. I lost my grandmother who was 73 years old. This was and still remains my own personal experience with genocide.

I am trying neither to shock nor to evoke sympathy. My purpose is to remind the reader that not unlike the Jews, the Ukrainians are a traumatized people who experienced this trauma individually and collectively. The twentieth century witnessed murder on a large scale and many nations fell victims to it, but in the first half of the century three nations stand out among all other victims of murder and genocide: the Armenians, the Jews, and, Yes, the Ukrainians.

Both Jews and Ukrainians revere their histories as oppressed people. It is not difficult to see that history has cast Jews and Ukrainians into many parallel situations and that there is a commonality of experiences between Jews and Ukrainians which is astonishing. And yet this commonality of experience does not translate itself into common efforts to achieve what should be equally shared objectives. The question arises, therefore, why is this so? And another one: how to resolve this question?

On my part the answer, to a degree, was the effort to write together with my friend Howard Aster the monograph *Jewish-Ukrainian Relations: Two Solitudes* and to organize the Conference on "Jewish-Ukrainian Relations in Historical Perspective."

AWAKENING FROM THE NIGHTMARE

James Joyce, an Irishman — and there are astonishing similarities between the Irish sensibility, and the Jewish sensibility, and the Ukrainian sensibility — in his monumental work *Ulysses* has Stephen Daedulus, the main protagonist, utter the phrase — "History is a nightmare from which I am trying to awake." For both Jews and Ukrainians, for both people, their own history is a nightmare. For both peoples, their histories are the story of oppression, brutalization by alien forces, the loss of statehood and the attempt to re-establish statehood, the aspirations to freedom. For Ukrainians, the agents of brutalization have been other slavic peoples — Poles, Russians, Hungarians, Tators. For Jews, the agents of brutalization, in the Ukrainian regions, were primarily Ukrainians. Whenever Ukrainians rose up in rebellion against their agents of oppression, Jews tended to be caught in the middle and suffered immensely. It is the irony of Jewish-Ukrainian relations that the very same figures who are the symbols of freedom for Ukrainians, such as Khmelntsky, are the figures of brutalization for Jews. The moments of valour for Ukrainians tend to be the moments of torment for Jews. The very invocation of the names of Khmelnytsky and Petlura awakes in the Jewish mind the memories of pogroms, murder, brutality — the most incandescent images of anti-semitism. These are the figures and the images which are inscribed in the collective memory of Jews. Is it any wonder, therefore, that for many Jews, Ukraine is a place from which Jews came, but it is the place that they want to forget? Is it any wonder, that scholars have shied away from the consideration of Jewish-Ukrainian relations? And, while there is no single Ukrainian perspective on the Jews, one of the most dominant views that appears to persist, even more strongly today, is that the Jews, although themselves an oppressed people, were an instrument of domination and oppression over the Ukrainians. It is this kind of thinking that has fueled the growing communal strife between the two communities in the past and does so, again, today.

But there is another side to history; those less dramatic moments when life progressed, communities thrived, prosperity abounded. And, in the ten centuries of recorded Jewish life in Ukraine, the Jewish community did thrive. It grew in numbers. It prospered. It spawned vigorous Hasidic movements. It developed a rich Yiddish literature. Indeed, when we look at Jewish life in Ukraine over these ten centuries we can see that during times of tranquility, Jewish life achieved some of its highest moments, in intellectual and cultural movements, in religious vigour, in material accomplishments. It is true that Jews and Ukrainians tended to live in separate domains, each community segregated from each other, with little contact or inter-relationship. There are sociological, economic and political reasons for this segregation. But what is important to remember is that the moments of dramatic confrontation between Jews and Ukrainians over ten centuries were limited and fairly short-termed. For the most part, Jews and Ukrainians over ten centuries were limited and fairly short-termed. For the most part, Jews and Ukrainians shared the same geographic territory in a condition of relative tranquility. And in some regions like in Transcarpathia, there were almost no conflicts between the two communities. Also in Galicia, until World War II, the competition between the two communities in the economic sphere did not prevent a great deal of cooperation in the political sphere.

Jews tend to think of the Jewish community in the Ukrainian region as an extension of the Jewish settlement patterns from Western Europe, into Eastern Europe, i.e. the push of German Jewry through the Polish Kingdom into the further eastern regions.

In actual fact, the earliest records of Jews in Ukrainian territories date back to the Second Century A.D. These Jews came to Crimea and the eastern shore of the Black Sea long before Christianity was introduced into the region. These Bosphorus and Middle Eastern Jews were highly Hellenized and they left behind them many inscriptions in Hebrew which date back to this period.

From Crimea and the Caucasus, Jews moved into the lower Volga and Don regions where the Khazar State, founded by the Turkic tribes, existed from the 7th to the 10th centuries. Around 740 Kahan Bulan and the Khazar elite even accepted Judaism as the state religion. The Khazar state ceased to exist shortly after its defeat by the Kiev prince Sviatoslav in 964. The Jews then migrated back to Crimea, the Caucasus and even into Rus'Ukraine.

Another fascinating event in early Jewish history in Ukraine took place in 987, when the Khazarian Jews proposed to Grand Duke Vladimir the Great of Kiev that he accept conversion to Judaism. The Chronicle describes how Prince Vladimir had presented to him arguments from representatives of three different religions — Byzantine Christianity, Roman Christianity and, significantly, Judaism.

Early Jewish history in the Ukraine also indicates that during the 11th and 12th centuries Jews lived in Kiev and had a separate district called "Zhydove," with a separate Jewish Gate to the district. There was an indentifiable Jewish community with a Jewish life in Ukraine as early as the 11th and 12th centuries and it persisted well into the 14th century. By that time, the entire region was in turmoil and we begin to see the movement of large numbers of Jews, coming from the Germanic regions, to settle into the Ukraine regions. From the 14th century onwards, we have a significantly different population base than during the previous period and we have the more familiar pattern of East European Jewry. But it is interesting to note that prior to this period, there was a Jewish population, small, but viable, with a different quality and cultural base in the Ukrainian regions, and it would appear that this early Jewish community in Ukraine had a fairly significant status and influence in the region.

But the turmoil of history tends to be stronger than the tranquility of history. For an historically oriented people, such as Jews, the brutality of history plays a vital role. Jews tend to retain their devotion to freedom because they remember their oppression. Jews are different from Stephen Daedulus. He tried to forget the nightmare of his own history. Jews try not to forget that history. If anything, they admonish anyone "lest they forget." In this obsession with the lessons of history, there is a profound lesson for Ukrainians.

Now let us return to Sir Karl Popper, himself an Austrian Jew. Karl Popper argues that fallibility is the hallmark of the human genius. Perfectability is not what signifies the highest of human achievements, rather it is the fact that we are prone to error, that we tend to make mistakes. What is vital is that we learn from those mistakes; that we never turn our backs on what it is to err; and to be truly human is to ensure than human error leads to human progress.

History cannot be re-written. It is unremitting, recalcitrant, it cannot be denied. But surely we can and we must learn from history. There are astonishing points of commonality between the aspirations, hopes and dreams of Jews and Ukrainians, especially today. What is it about the common history of Jews and Ukrainians that we can learn, which can serve as a basis for some common approaches to problems?

First, it is in the interest of both Jews and Ukrainians to be at the forefront in the struggle for human rights, especially within the U.S.S.R. The fact is that many Jews and Ukrainians have shared common prison cells in the U.S.S.R. over the past years because they have linked arms in the struggle for human rights. This is an issue which is urgent in the context of East European and Soviet societies.

Second, the struggle for the retention of the 'right to one's own language and culture' — enshrined as it is in the United Nations Charter on Human Rights — is another issue which united Jews and Ukrainians today. Russification, the espoused policy of the U.S.S.R. towards its Republics, affects all Ukrainians and the 800,000 Jews who still live in Ukraine today.

The editors of the clandestine *Ukrains'kyi Visnyk* (7-8, 1974) in their polemic with Shcherbytskj, First Secretary of the Communist Party of Ukraine, and in demonstration of respect for all peoples and in rejection of crude chauvinisms, asked pointedly: "Why primarily of the Russian people, language and culture and not of the German people and its extremely rich spiritual and material culture, and the German language — the language of Marx and Engels? Why not of the talented, much suffering Jewish people, whose history so closely resembles Ukrainian history, especially during its tragic moments? Why not of the brotherly Polish people? Why not of the English language which is really the most international language? Why not in equal measure, of all the peoples of the earth which is not so vast as it once was?"

The very same sentiments and arguments were expressed by Ivan Dzyuba in his powerful speech at the ceremonies at Babyn Iar." "Jews have the right to be Jews, Ukrainians the right to be Ukrainians, in the most complete and profound sense of these words. Let the Jews learn Jewish history, culture, language and be proud of them. Let both peoples know each other's history and culture and the history and culture of other peoples. Let them know how to esteem themselves and others — as their brothers." The very same themes were voiced poetrically by the greatest of Ukrainian poets, Taras Shevchenko: "to learn from others, but to cherish our own."

Third, in a world dominated by empires, super-powers and the prerogatives of imperial rule — now called spheres of influence — the fate of small nations is increasingly precarious. One need not remind people of the precariousness of the fate of the State of Israel as an example. In the contestations of empires in the contemporary world, small nations must begin to recognize their common interests and to lend support one to another. In this areas, as well, Ukrainians and Jews share a common interest, namely to ensure that the right to national self-preservation and statehood is recognized and supported.

Fourth, and perhaps most importantly, we must recognize that in the struggles of people for freedom, nobody should sit on the sidelines, nobody should turn their backs on one another. The struggle of communities and peoples to survive, to achieve a condition of freedom involves all of our. The horror of human indifference to oppression and brutalization must not be relived.

Jews and Ukrainians have a common stake in ensuring that this sort of horror not be relived. We must learn from our common history that he who sits on the sidelines of history becomes the accomplice of indifference.

But what about Jews and Ukrainians in Canada? There are radicals and moderates, orthodox and conservative, progressive and regressive elements in both the Jewish and Ukrainian communities in Canada. Both communities have significant population centres concentrated in specific cities. Both communities in Canada tend to be looked upon as senior partners in the multicultural complexion of the Canadian nation.

It appears to us that some very powerful links between Jews and Ukrainians can be built here in Canada. One of the reasons for this possibility is the fact that Ukrainians have a profound admiration for Jews in Canada — for their achievements in various fields of endeavour, for their historical positions on important issues which affect other ethnic communities. And, they have admiration for Jews because they look at Jews and they want to emulate them — surprising, but true! To Ukrainians, Jews are fellow travellers in a diaspora. Ukrainians look upon the Jews and they say to themselves — "look at those people — they too were oppressed, robbed of their homeland, but they survived in the diaspora and they finally achieved their statehood." And in Canada, Ukrainians look at Jews and they see the incredibly successful community institutions which Jews have established over the years — newspapers, hospitals, schools, youth clubs, summer camps, old peoples' homes. Ukrainians look at all this and they want to do the same. To the Ukrainian community, Jews in Canada have achieved a position of high development in community institutions — and they want to achieve the same.

There is also another dimension to the relatedness of Jews and Ukrainians in Canada. As one of the oldest, most established community in Canada, Jews are expected to and do provide leadership for many communities on a wide variety of issues, but particularly in the area of human rights. The Ukrainian has been a leading force in Canada in the constitutional entrenchment of the multicultural heritage of Canadians. it seems, therefore, logical that the concerns of both communities could be joined to the general profit for all Canadians. Because we in Canada, as a society, believe that human rights cannot be achieved individually unless group rights are recognized, as well. My liberty is conjoined to the liberty of my community. Professor and now judge Walter Tarnopolsky put it well when he said: "Unless one bases one's attitude on respect and love of human being for human being, unless one accepts that the deprivation of human rights of anyone, anywhere, is a deprivation of humanity which then in turn affects me, we are not going to achieve anything for any of us."

This attitude of respect grows, it flourishes in cooperative understandings, in joint projects, in better understanding between our two communities, our two peoples. But the first and the most important step is that we have to start talking to each other.

Every idea has its time — or so it seems. The thoughts that may be unthinkable or heretical to one generation may become commonplace and acceptable to another generation. At least among intellectuals and in the academic community, one hopes that there is enough courage to take on those unusual ideas and to consider them carefully, dispassionately and with self-critical candor.

For some years now, academics in various countries have had the courage to suggest that it may be the propitious time to undertake a discussion of the question of Jewish-Ukrainian relations. A number of efforts, on an individual and collaborative basis have been undertaken. A number of small-scale meetings, discussions and publoic conferences have taken place in various settings. But more should be done and not simply by scholars but also by community leaders, politicians, youth groups and church leaders. Yes, we believe the time for Jewish-Ukrainian dialogue has arrived.

Lord Byron, we think, said: "there is nothing so difficult as a beginning." He was addressing the question of poetry. But in intellectual matters, especially in relation to the question of Jewish-Ukrainian relations, the saying is equally true!

INDEX

Adelheim, Ye., 29
Agro-Joint, 27
Agursky, M., 40
Aleichem, Sholom, 29, 44
Alexander II, 58
Alexander, Edward, 40, 43
Almond, Gabriel A., 17
America, 59
American Jewish Committee, 15
Ami, Ben, 62
Anarchists, 27
Anti-Semitisim, 13, 14, 40, 41, 42, 59
Antonenko-Davydovych, B., 32
Aptekman, Joseph, 58
Arenda, 24, 25
Armenia, 23
Armenians, 69
Ash, Sholom, 29
Attwood, Margaret, 12
Austria, 37
Austria-Hungary, 26, 31, 36-37, 60, 65-66
Avramovych Family, 25
Avramovych, Mark, 24
Babi, Yar, 13, 35
Bacon, Francis, 20, 29
Baltic Sea, 36
Bantish-Kamenskyi, D., 61
Barochov, Ben, 58, 67
Baron, Solo W., 53, 54
Beilis Trial, 30
Ben-Sasson, H.H., 53, 55
Benedict, Ruth, 16
Berger, Abraham, 38
Bergeron, Leandre, 12
Berlin, 29, 56
Bielo-Russia, 68
Bikel, Sh., 29
Bilinsky, Yaroslav, 19
Bilu Society, 58
Birnbaum, N., 29
Birobidzhan, 27
Black Death in Western Europe, 43
Black Sea, 21, 36
Bohemia, 37
Boleslaw, Duke of Kalisz, 37
Bolshevik Regime, 67
Bolsheviks, 27, 33
Borokhovych, M. (1687-1704), 24
Borshchakivskyi, O., 29
Borulliak, T., 32
Borys, Jury, 64
Boryslav, 26
Brouwer, Martin, 20
Bryan, Robert J., 55
Bukovina, 29, 60
Bulan, Kahan, 21
Bund, 26, 32-33, 67
Bundism, 60
Byzantine Christianity, 22
Canada, 11, 51
Casimir The Great (1333-1370), 23, 37
Catherine II, 25
Catholic Poland, 61
Catholics, 37
Caucasus, 21
Central Europe, 43, 57, 66, 69
Central Ukrainian Council (Rada), 68
Chair of Jewish History & Literature, 27
Chazan, Robert, 45
Cheka, 33
Chornovil, V., 35
Christianity, 30
Church Slavonic, 61
Collectivization Of Agriculture, 27
Colonel of Hadiach, 24
Colonel of Poltava, 24
Cook, Ramsay, 12

Cossack Starshyna, 25
Cossack Uprising, 28
Cossacks, 44
Council of Great Poland, Little Poland..., 23
Council of Great Poland ... Red Rus' & Volhynia, 23
Council of Lithuania, 23
Council of Ukr. Peoples Rep., 26
Cracow, 28
Crimea, 21-22, 27, 36
Crusades In Western Europe, 43
Cultural Development, 28
Czechoslovakia, 27
Danylo, King of Halych-Volhynia, 22
Dawidowicz, Lucy S., 13, 17, 56, 58
Decembrist Uprising, 57
Deutscher, Isaac, 41, 44
Diadychenko, V.A., 64
Diaspora Ukrainians, 35
Diaspora, 34, 43,46
Don, 21
Doroshenko, D., 60
Drahomanov, M.P., (1841-1895), 61, 62
Dubnov, 67
Dubnow, Simon, 23, 37-40, 42-43, 67
Dubrovs'kyi, V., 63
Duke Boleslaw of Kalisz, 37
Dushnyk, W., 15, 19, 23-24
Dzyuba, Ivan, 35
East Europe, 31-32, 55, 57, 59, 66, 69
East-Central Europe, 57
Eastern European Jews, 24, 56
Ecumenism, 15
English Canadians, 11
English-Canadian Perspective, 12
Erasmus, 30

Estonia, 68
Ettinger, S., 53, 55
Europe, 51, 58-60
European Jewry, 44
Fedenko, Panas, 27
Feldman, Leon A., 53
Fischer, John, 14
Frankel, Jonathan Charles, 51, 59, 62, 67
Franko, Ivan, 32, 43, 63
Freidorf, 27
French-Canadian Perspective, 12
French-Canadians, 11
Frug, Sholom, 29
Frye, Northrop, 12
Gaboury, Jean-Pierre, 12
Galicia, 23, 27, 60, 65
Galician Stage, 61
Geneva Stage, 61
Gentile World, 41-42
German Emperor Maximillian I, 23
German Nationalisim, 56
Germans, 14
Germany, 23, 37, 62
Gezerah of 1648, 38, 43
Gogol, N., 32
Goldelman, Solomon I., 26, 27, 34, 67-68
Gorer, Geoffrey, 17
Gpu, 33
Grand Duke Vladimir The Great of Kiev, 22
Grayzel, Solomon, 45
Great Catastrophe, 39
Greek Orthodox Ukrainians, 38
Greek Orthodox Christianity, 30
Greenberg, Louis, 58
Gronsky, P., 63
Gross, Nochum, 57
Grouix, Abbe Lionel, 12
Haam, Achad, Kievan Jew (1856-1927), 28

Haboleh, Kievan Rabbi Moses (1448–1529), 28
Haidamak Uprisings, 25
Haliv, M., 14
Halych, 23
Haman, 43
Hanover, Nathan Nata, 39
Hasidism, 56–57
Haskalah, 56–57, 59
Hebrew, 28, 58
Hegel, Georg Wilhelm Friedrich, 47
Heifetz, 35
Herasymenko, M., 63
Herbil'S'Kyi, H., 60
Hermaize, J., 26, 29
Hermaize, O., 60
Hertsyk, P. (1675–1695), 24
Hertzberg, Arthur, 53
Herzl, Theodore, 32
Hetmanshchyna, 25
Himka, John–Paul, 62
Historical Record, 19
Hitler, 43
Holland, 28
Holocaust, 43–45
Holovanivskyi, S., 29
Horowitz, B., 29
Hosenpud, A., 29
Hrushevskyi, Mykhailo, 22, 60
Hrymailo, Ia., 32
Hunczak, Taras, 19
Hungary, 30
Hurzhii, I., 63
Iavors'Kyi, M., 60
Idola, 30, 39, 47
Ievdokimenko, V. Iu., 16, 35
Ihnatov, V.O., 16, 35
Ilnytskyi, R., 15
Imperial Russian Government, 62
Islam, 30
Israel, 34–35, 45–46

Istoriia Rusov, 61
Iukhvid, L., 29
Iurovska, L., 29
Jewish Autonomy, 26, 67
Jewish Batallion, 27
Jewish Chroniclers, 24, 43
Jewish Colonies, 27
Jewish Community, 54–57, 69
Jewish Homeland, 27, 34
Jewish Ministry of Government, 34
Jewish Minority, 42
Jewish Movements, 41
Jewish National Areas, 27
Jewish National Autonomy, 34, 67–69
Jewish National Council, 27, 68
Jewish National Life, 62
Jewish Nationalism, 58
Jewish People's Party, 26
Jewish Populist, 58
Jewish Schools, 27
Jewish Workers Party, 26
Jewish-Polish Relations, 51
Jewish-Russian Relations, 51
Jewish-Ukrainian Cooperation, 36, 60
Jewish-Ukrainian Dialogue, 36
Jewish-Ukrainian Relations, 11, 13, 16–19, 42, 45–48, 52–53, 55, 65–66, 69–70
Jews, 21, 24–25, 27–32, 35–42, 44–48, 51, 54–55, 57–60, 62, 66–67, 69–70
Joyce, James, 47, 52
Judaism, 22, 30, 36
Kaczurowskyj, I., 32
Kagan, V., 15
Kalinindorf, 27
Kaminskyi, A., 14
Kann, Ri, 63
Karaites, 25
Karavanskyi, V., 35

Katsnelson, A., 29
Katz, Jacob, 54-56
Kehillot, 23, 57
Keiman, Leo, 14
Kharkov Stage, 61
Kharkov, 14, 64
Khazar State, 21-22, 36
Kherson, 27
Khmelnytsky, Bohdan, 23, 24, 38-40, 43-44
Khmelnytskyi Uprising, 38
Khvyliovyi, M., 32
Kichko, 35
Kiev Stage, 61
Kiev, 22-23, 26, 35, 62
Kirgizia, 62
Kleiner, Izrajil, 19
Kokhba, 43
Koliivshchyna, 25
Kolomyia, 29
Kompaniets, I., 64
Komshtein, A., 29
Kononenko, K., 63
Korchma, 31
Korn, Rachel, 29
Kostomarov, N., 62
Kotliarevskyi, Ivan, 61
Kotsiubynaskyi, M., 32
Krasnyi, P., 26
Krevets'Kyi, A., 63
Kroeber, A.L., 17
Kryvyi, Rih, 27
Kubiiovych, V., 21
Kulish, P., 62
Kulyk, I.,29
Kurylo, O., 29
Kivtkovs'Kyi, O. Mytsiuk, 63
Latvia, 68
Latzki-Bertold, W., 39
Left-Bank Ukraine, 25
Leites, A., 29
Leshchenko, N., 63

Levesque, Rene, 12
Levyts'Kyi, K., 60
Levytskyi, Zh. M., 32
Lieberman, Aaron, 58
Linton, Ralph, 16
Lippmann, Walter, 20
Lithuanian Principality, 23, 68
Lithuanian Statues of 1529, 1566, 1589, 23
Liubchenko, A., 32
Los', F.E., 64
Lviv, 27
MacLennan, Hugh, 11, 13
Magna Carta, 37
Makhno, N., 27
Maksymovych, M., 61
Mandel, Eli, 12
Margolin, A., 26
Margulis, Z., 26
Markevych, M., 61
Markovych Family, 25
Marxism, 64
Maskilim, 57
Maximillian I, German Emperor, 23
McRoberts, Kenneth, 12
Mead, Margaret, 17
Medieval Polish Jewry, 37
Memmi, Albert, 42, 44
Mendelsohn, Ezra, 55
Messiah, 43, 44
Messianic Movement, 43
Methodological Problems, 16
Metropolitan Ilarion, 22
Metropolitan Stephan Sulyk, 15
Middle Eastern Jews, 21
Millner, Henry, 12
Millner, Sheilagh Hodgins, 12
Ministry of Jewish Affairs, 27, 68
Mintz, M., 67
Mishkinsky, Moshe, 55
Moicher-Sforim, Mendele, 29

Moroz, V., 35
Moses, 32
Multiculturalism, 66
Muscovite Orthodoxy, 30
Muscovites, 24
Myrnyi, P., 32
National Autonomy, 33
National Character, 16-17, 29
National Minorities, 28
National-Personal Autonomy, 26
Nazi Collaborators, 35
Nazi Propaganda, 14
Nazis, 28, 35, 43, 69
Nesterenko, O., 63
Nicholas, I., 57, 58
Nkvd, 33
Non-Soviet Eastern Europe, 67
Non-Ukrainians, 31
North America, 29
Novhorod-Siversk, 60
Novyi Zlatopil, 27
Odessa, 26
Ogpu, 33
Ohloblyn, O., 63
Okhrymovych, V., 60
Oles, O., 32
Olifovich, M., 29
Orenstein, Ia., 29
Orlyk, Hetman Philip, 24
Orthodox Russia, 61
Orthodox Ukrainians, 25
Osechyns'Syi, V., 63
Ostapenko, S., 63
Ottoman Empire, 30, 43
Oun, 28
Pale of Settlement, 25
Palestine, 14, 58
Paris Peace Treaties, 67
Pavlovskyi, O., 61
Pavluk Rebellion of 1637, 23
Pervomaiskyi, L., 29, 32
Peter The Great, 25

Petliura, Simon, 19
Pharaohs, 43
Philadelphia, 15
Philosophy of History, 52
Pidhaini, Oleg, 14
Plato, 20
Poalei-Zion, 26
Podolia, 26, 56
Pogroms of 1881, 59
Pogroms, 26-27, 37, 59
Poland, 23, 25, 27, 36, 60
Poland-Lithuania, 23
Poles, 24, 27, 31, 37, 39
Poletyka, J., 61
Poliakov, Leon, 30
Polish Catholicism, 30
Polish Kingdom, 36-37, 39, 53
Polish Magnates, 37
Polish-Ukrainian Conflict, 27
Political Culture, 17
Populist Movement, 58
Porits'Kyi, A., 64
Possony, Stephan T., 25, 40
Postgate, Dale, 12
Potichnyj, P.J., 28
Predjudice, 13
Pritsak, O., 60-61
Prokhor, Monk, 22
Promised Land, 34
Prosvitas (Enlightenment Societies), 31, 64
Protocols of the Elders of Zion, 33
Public Com., for Jew.-Ukr. Coop., 14-15
Pye, Lucian W., 17
Pypin, A., 60
Quebec, 12
Rabbinic Judaism, 56
Rabinovich, Shmul, 29
Rada, 34
Rafes, M., 26
Raisin, Jacob S., 55

Raphael, Marc Lee, 45
Religious Freedom, 28
Rempel, Rachel, 11
Reshetar, Jr., J.S., 60-61, 64
Revolution, 1917, 65
Revolutionary Ukrainina Party, 64
Revutsky, A., 26
Rickman, John, 17
Right-Bank Ukraine, 25
Rignel'Man, O., 61
Rivkin, Ellis, 51, 53
Roman Christianity, 22
Romania, 27
Rothschild, Joseph, 46
Rudanskyj, S., 32
Rudnytsky, I.L., 60-62
Rus'-Ukraine, 22-23, 30
Russia, 25, 36, 60, 62-64
Russian Black Hundreds, 26
Russian Christianity, 30
Russian Empire, 25-26, 32, 51, 56, 58, 65-66
Russian Revolution, 42, 68
Russian Serfs, 58
Russians, 25, 37
Russification, 35, 62, 69
Rybak, N., 29
Statute of 1334, 23
Savchenko, F., 60
Schapiro, Leonard, 32-33
Schwartz, Harry, 14
Schwartz, Solomon M., 14
Second Grand Assembly of the Oun, 28
Shchoholiv, Ia., 32
Shchupak, S., 29
Sheptytsky, Metropolitan A., 28
Shevchenko, Taras, 32, 61-62
Shtendera, Ye., 28
Shul'Ha I., 64
Shulvass, M.A., 36, 39-40
Sich Sharpshooters, 27

Singer, Isaac B., 40, 43-44
Skoropadsky, Hetman I., 25
Slabchenko, M., 63
Slobozhanshchyna, 25
Smilanskyi, L., 29
Smolych, Iu., 32
Socialist-Revolutionaries, 64
Society of Jewish-Ukrainian Relations, 14
Society of Saints Cyril and Methodius, 62
Southern Ukraine (Novorossiiskaia Gubernia), 25, 36
Soviet Dictatorship, 13
Soviet Domination, 48
Soviet Jews, 46-47
Soviet Nationalities Policies, 69
Soviet Union, 15
Spektor, Sh., 15
Stalin, I.V., 29, 69
Stalindorf, 27
Stalinist Policies, 69
Starshyna, 24
Statute of National-Personal Autonomy, 68
Stebelskyi, I., 14
Stebun, I., 29
Stereotype, 20
Survival, 12
Survivance, 12
Suslensky, Yakov, 15, 35
Sutherland, Ronald, 12
Sverdlov, Ia., 33
Sviatopolk, Prince, 22
Switzerland, 62
Szajkowski, Zosa, 19
Szporluk, R., 61-62
Tanenbaum, Joseph, 14
Tanenbaum, Rabbi Marc, 15
Taras Bortherhood (Bratstvo Tarasivtsiv), 64
Tatars, 36

Tcherikower, Ellias, 19
Teplyts'Kyi, V., 63
Third Extraordinary Grand
  Assembly of the Oun, 28, 34
Tobias, Henry J., 55
Tohobochnyi, I., 32
Toryn, V., 29
Transcarpathia, 60
Treadgold, D.W., 61
Treaty of Andrusovo (1667), 25
Troianker, R., 29
Trotsky, L., 33
Tsar Nicholas I, 57
Tsarist Government, 26, 30, 33
Tsarist Police, 62
Turkey, 43
Turkic Tribes, 21
Two Solitudes, 11, 47
U.N. Charter of Human Rights, 70
U.S.S.R., 70
Ukazes of 1727, 1738, 1740, 1741,
  1742, 1785, 25
Ukraine, 23-27, 29-32, 35-39,
  47-48, 51, 53-54, 60-63, 65,
  67-68, 70
Ukrainian Catholic Church, 15, 25
Ukrainian Central Rada, 26, 33
Ukrainian Community, 55, 69
Ukrainian Culture, 36
Ukrainian Diaspora, 35
Ukrainian Folklore, 30
Ukrainian Galician Army (UHA),
  27
Ukrainian Guerillas, 27
Ukrainian Haidamaks, 38
Ukrainian Independence, 60-70
Ukrainian Insurgent Army, 28
Ukrainian Kozaks, 39
Ukrainian Language, 62
Ukrainian Movements, 42
Ukrainian Nation State, 36
Ukrainian National Character, 62

Ukrainian Nationalism, 35
Ukrainian Parties, 26
Ukrainian Party of Social
  Federalists, 26
Ukrainian Peasantry, 54
Ukrainian People's Council, 27
Ukrainian Peoples Party, 64
Ukrainian Peoples Republic, 27
Ukrainian Perspective, 29
Ukrainian Political Movement, 62
Ukrainian Press, 29
Ukrainian Revolution, 68
Ukrainian Social Democratic
  Workers' Party, 26, 64
Ukrainian SSR, 27, 46
Ukrainian State, 68
Ukrainian-Polish Conflict, 39
Ukrainians, 28-30, 35-37, 39, 42,
  46-48, 51, 54, 62, 66-67, 69
Unkrainka, L., 32
Ukrainian National Revival, 60
Union of Lublin (1569), 23
United Nations Declaration
  of Human Rights, 47
United States, 45-46, 51, 59
University of Kamenets-Podolsk,
  27
USSR, 35, 46
Vaads, 23
Vasylkovych, Vladimir, 22
Vatican Council II, 15
Verba, Sidney, 17
Vertep, 31
Veselovskyi, B., 63
Vidrodzhennia Society, 31
Vienna Parliament, 26
Volga, 21
Volhynia, 22, 26, 56
Volianska, L., 15
Vulf-Liatsky, Ia., 26
Vynnychenko, V., 32
Wade, Mason, 12

West, 23
Western (Latin) Christianity, 30
Western Europe, 22, 28, 30, 32, 56
Western Ukrainian People's Republic, 27
White Russian Armies, 27
Weirzynski, Joseph L., 62
Witte, Count, 32
Wittenberg, Solomon, 58
World Congress of Free Ukrainians, 35
World War I, 60
World War II, 27-28, 38, 44-45, 60, 69

Yiddish Literature, 40, 48
Yiddish, 23, 27-29, 34, 60, 62
Zaporozhian Sich, 25
Zarycky, G.B., 15
Zhabotynskyi, V., 19
Zhitlovsky, 67
Zhydove, 22
Zilberfarb, M., 26
Zionism, 32-35, 45, 60
Zionists, 26, 35
Zolotarev, O., 26